Hawaii Recalls

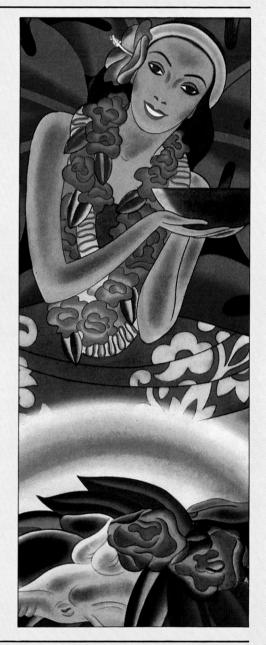

Selling Romance to America

Nostalgic Images of the Hawaiian Islands:
1910 • 1950

Text by DeSoto Brown • Design by Anne Ellett
Photography by Gary Giemza

An Editions Limited Book

Published by Editions Limited, 111 Royal Circle, Honolulu, Hawaii 96816

Library of Congress Catalog Card Number 82-83322

ISBN 0-9607938-2-8 (softcover)

First Printing 1982
Second Printing 1984
Third Printing 1987
Printed in Singapore

Typesetting by Studio Graphics - Honolulu, Hawaii
Cover Art by Charles Valoroso from an original design by Frank MacIntosh.

If you have any information or inquiries concerning Hawaii Recalls please write to P.O. Box 61405, Honolulu, Hawaii 96822-8405

Contents

so this is hawaii

S o this is Hawaii...? Well, no, it really isn't. And it never was Hawaii either, not even in the good old days.

This book is all about fantasy. It's a depiction of Hawaii that was developed over a period of about 40 years by people who were promoting the islands. During this time —from about 1910 up through the 1950's—an imaginary version of Hawaii was fabricated by the businesses that really needed to make the rest of the country and the world aware of the islands: the steamship companies and airlines, the tour guide and car rental firms, and even the pineapple growers and alohawear manufacturers. They (and the Territory of Hawaii itself) all came to increasingly depend on tourism for their economic

well-being, and everyone knew that creating a good reputation and keeping it strong were essential for success. They were selling romance, not just repeating facts, in the torrent of printed matter on the subject; from hand-tinted postcards to small brochures to large colorful booklets, all extolling Hawaii and its products.

And Hawaii wasn't used in just brochures and other giveaway promotional items, for the islands turned up in magazine articles (both for tourist information and as the subjects of serious, newsworthy pieces) as well as in books for both children and adults. Writers could utilize Hawaii as an exotic backdrop for their stories, or they could delve into "what made Hawaii tick"—that spot so far away from

the rest of the country and yet so much like it, a place with an apparently American veneer that hid mysterious inner workings. Such writings were especially common before World War II, when the Pacific area seemed dangerously close to war and Hawaii was "America's first line of defense". What would the largely Oriental population do in the event war broke out? Such investigative reporting sidestepped the carefree image so carefully cultivated for the rest of the world by Hawaii's promoters.

For the many people who were uninterested in reading, there were always Hollywood movies, and even photographs taken in the islands gracing their Sunday newspapers. Films used Hawaii for all sorts of celluloid action, from tap-dancing hula girls and angry volcanoes to murder mysteries and communist plots. These weren't strictly intended to promote the islands as such, but they helped to do the job nonetheless. The fact that these movies were usually utterly unrealistic bolstered, instead of diminished, their selling abilities.

Hawaii was also given a boost economically when, every so often, the islands become a fad. Such crazes pop up from time to time, the way these things happen, often because of a news event — either bad (the Pearl Harbor attack, 1941) or good (statehood, 1959). Or sometimes Hawaii comes into style for no readily identifiable reason, as with the Hawaiian music fads of 1915-'20 or the late 1930's. Whatever the cause, a fashion for Hawaii among people elsewhere is usually cause for pleased business people in the islands.

Most of the pictures you'll see in Hawaii Recalls are the romanticized illustrations that appeared in printed matter about the islands. Nowadays, such commercial artwork has been replaced by photography and is only rarely encountered. But it's a useful technique when one is trying to create a fanciful, pleasant impression, which is what most of Hawaii's promoters were working for. Perhaps its basic unreality has given it a slightly looked-down-upon position in the art world, where fine art is praised and commercial art (regardless of the talent or ability involved) is ignored. Commercial art never has the freedom of expression that fine art does, since it must always play up its subject's good points. But it's valid nonetheless, and deserves the serious attention that it has usually been denied.

Accompanying these marvelous illustrations are quotes from contemporary sources. Many are just as extravagantly overstated as the pictures are, but occasionally reality might intrude from a writer not impressed by the claims he or she had been innundated with. And even those skeptics usually ended up being just as impressed with the islands as anyone else — in spite of their misgivings over the sometimes excessive boosterism they encountered.

What is the aim of Hawaii Recalls? Mainly to show you the work of those people in the past who invented the dream paradise of Hawaii. Certainly much of what is contained in this book is unrealistic. But then, a little fantasy never hurt anyone. It has, in fact, entertained a great many people. The hope is that the words and illustrations collected here will manage to transport you to a tropical island heaven where hula girls strum their ukuleles under the moonlit palms, and "care and worry are 'taboo'". Then you'll be joining the millions of people who still cherish this ideal of Hawaii — an ideal created by the designers of the elements presented in Hawaii Recalls.

The Setting

T here is one fact about Hawaii that no one can dispute: it is very beautiful. Not only is its weather divinely soothing (a happy result of its being placed just right in the Pacific Ocean), but it also is graced with scenery that ranges from the calmly peaceful to the exhilarating and spectacular. Rich tropical vegetation delights the eye (and sometimes the nose as well, when the islands' countless flowers come into bloom), while beneath the surface of the sea swim dazzlingly-colored fish. Even the skies above the islands are exciting to view, filled as they are with brilliant rainbows and gorgeous sunsets and, at night, a moon that seems to be hung there for romance.

Perhaps you, as a modern-day reader, find the preceeding account a bit overdone. Thirty or forty years ago, though, this was the usual style in which the natural attributes of Hawaii were described. These natural features of the islands are the subject of this first chapter; the aspects of paradise that no human being can take credit for. Hawaii is indeed fortunate to have all these things. Were it not for the weather and the scenery that the islands offer, Hawaii would never have achieved its desired status in the world. No amount of promotion would have caught anyone's eye if the basic attractions hadn't been there in the first place to be promoted.

Probably there have always been doubters in the world, for whom a flowery description of anything or anyplace will be a signal to disbelieve. They are the types who, upon actually arriving in Hawaii, point out how unimpressive Diamond Head is and how they've seen better sunsets elsewhere. Even this kind of visitor, however, can be won over eventually by what we're calling Hawaii's "setting", which pictures and words never really succeed in fully describing.

(FACING PAGE): Cover of postcard holder, 1930's.

H awaii. Mention the word and the average person would think of a tropical island far away in the South Pacific - which would, of course, be totally wrong for two reasons. First, Hawaii is located <u>above</u> the equator, putting it in the North Pacific - which unfortunately doesn't sound as warm and exotic. And second, although there is <u>an</u> island named Hawaii, it is just one of the whole group that carries the same name. To make it clear that there was more than one island awaiting you, Hawaii's promoters created maps. And, also, the curving island chain has always been a nice motif to use for its own sake, like the design on the cover of <u>The Story of Hawaii</u>, from about 1930 (**LOWER RIGHT**).

It was always hoped that the visitor could be enticed to move from isle to isle and thus spread the wealth. To this end, a trend began in the 1920's of using frivolous maps to show the unique features of the outer islands (or "neighbor islands", as they came to be called in a more friendly manner). Each island is different and does have its own beauty spots, but the tendency has always been for tourists to get to Oahu and stay put for the whole time they're in Hawaii. This 1931 advertisement (**FACING PAGE**) tries to convey how much fun would be missed were the traveller to omit a little island-hopping from his itinerary. Including cartoon-like human beings disporting themselves in a multitude of festive ways was a typical style of the 1920's, and was useful and cute enough to be carried on for some years.

". . . that palm-fringed handful of islands carelessly strewn in a random arc in mid-Pacific, like the last grains from a weary sower's hand."

Roaming in Hawaii, 1937

SEE HAWAII

MATSON NAVIGATION CO.
SAN FRANCISCO — HONOLULU
DIRECT TO VOLCANO

he islands of Hawaii are actually the tops of great mountains that rise up from the floor of the Pacific. They were created volcanically, and the still-active craters of the island of Hawaii are a most unusual and promotion-worthy aspect of paradise. Just such a luridly glowing firepit adorns the front of a postcard folder from 1943 **(BELOW)**. Since Hawaiian volcanoes have only rarely erupted explosively in modern times, they can be looked upon as exciting (and courteously benign) novelties instead of dangers.

Erupting volcanoes are so commonplace in the islands that these two ladies can just strum their ukuleles and look the other way as smoke rises in the background - a Matson Navigation Company postcard maiden **(LEFT)** and a calendar girl **(FACING PAGE)**, both from the 1920's.

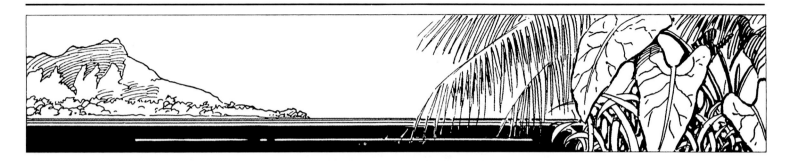

ow could there be a book about Hawaii without a picture or two (or more) of Diamond Head? There couldn't be, so presented herewith is the world-famed mountain in a variety of views. **(THIS PAGE)**: a line drawing from a 1933 Paradise of the Pacific magazine **(TOP)**, and a detail from some rayon fabric manufactured in Japan in the 1950's **(RIGHT)**. Facing page: the Love's Bakery Real Hawaiian Fruit Cake tin **(NEAR RIGHT)**, was used from the 1920's through the 1950's and was perfect for sending a taste of the tropics to family and friends on the mainland. The surfer gazing pensively at Diamond Head in the dusk **(FAR RIGHT)** is thinking that "giant 4-engine United Mainliner 300s now speed across the Pacific to this island paradise in just a few short hours," or so the message printed on the back of this 1950's postcard might have you think.

"*Diamond Head crouches like a headless sphinx with its paws in the sea guarding Honolulu.*"

Colorful Hawaii, 1945

LOVE'S REAL HAWAIIAN FRUIT CAKE

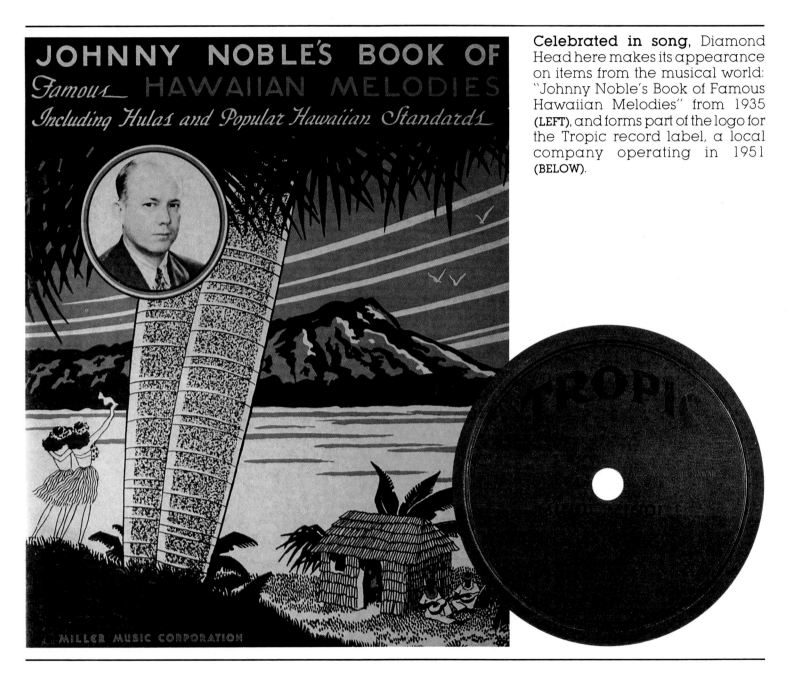

Celebrated in song, Diamond Head here makes its appearance on items from the musical world: "Johnny Noble's Book of Famous Hawaiian Melodies" from 1935 **(LEFT)**, and forms part of the logo for the Tropic record label, a local company operating in 1951 **(BELOW)**.

Diamond Head is considered a rather romantic sight, seeming to speak of love. Here it's the background **(RIGHT)** for the usual interracial couple on the cover of a piece of sheet music from 1916. In reality, though, the area around Diamond Head (including the Kaimuki district, where the "Sweet Brown Maid" hails from) was dry and scrubby with a few farms and dairies at that time - not what one would expect of a land so rich in romance. A reminder of those days is the milk bottle cap **(ABOVE)** from around 1950, a relic of a long-vanished agricultural scene in what are now crowded suburbs.

The von Hamm Young Co. Ltd.
HONOLULU - HAWAII

"*Diamond Head is the true symbol of Hawaii and one of the most readily identifiable landmarks on earth. Its likeness may be found on purple sateen pillow slips, framing a poem about Mother, branded into wallets, printed on aloha shirts, embossed on compacts, engraved on ukuleles, carved from Hawaiian woods and pictured on souvenir dinnerware.*" Waikiki Beachnik, 1960

About two million years after most of the island of Oahu had appeared above the waves and was weathering quietly, a group of vigorous small volcanoes burst out along its southern coast. Diamond Head was one of these young upstarts. Its distinctive shape, with the 761-foot peak at the right, was created during its last eruptions when the prevailing trade winds blew the ejected cinders in that direction. It certainly wasn't built by major eruptions, as these things go, and if Diamond Head were not situated as the backdrop to an equally famous beach, it probably never would have won a second glance from anyone.

As stewardesses on interisland planes are heard to announce as you fly past it, "Diamond Head received its name in the 19th century, when visiting British sailors found sparkling crystals on its slopes, and thought them to be diamonds." The calcite crystals they actually found were worth nothing, but almost ever since that time the name and image of Diamond Head have been put to fullest use in the promotion of Hawaii's businesses. Here it serves as the design for a 1928 ad for a local corporation (LEFT).

"...the setting is extravagantly beautiful, with Diamond Head thrusting its bulk out into the opal sea..."

Our Hawaii, 1942

People have used Diamond Head for a variety of purposes. Ancient Hawaiians, it is said, committed human sacrifices on its slopes. A lookout on its ocean side proved a convenient spot for sharp-eyed men in the 1800's to watch for incoming ships so that a fast rider could gallop to town to announce an imminent arrival. Modern American military fortifications ("the strongest in the islands") were installed in Diamond Head in the early years of this century, and up through World War II there was talk of the slightly mysterious tunnelings and equipment that civilians were not allowed to see. None of this, however, was ever used for the defense of Honolulu. Above and beyond all such activities, though, Diamond Head's most profitable use will always continue to be as an easily-remembered trademark for Hawaii; one which by now is imprinted in the minds of millions.

Check over all these pictures of Diamond Head once more and you'll see that it is an unwritten law that there be a palm tree or two included, preferably on the left. Nowadays you're more likely to see a highrise or two in this scene instead of a palm, but even if the view of Diamond Head from Waikiki has been almost totally obscured you can still recapture the image of that famous profile by looking at any of a thousand representations of Diamond Head still in use.

Here are two oldies: a 1924 Paradise of the Pacific magazine cover **(RIGHT)** and a fantasy setting from Kimo **(BELOW)**, from 1928, which features not only the obligatory palms but the rising sun as well, in a position that it never occupies in reality.

"It is the mist falling when the sun is bright. . . that arches the haze of purple valleys with brilliant rainbows so close that one can almost touch them. . ."

The Story of Hawaii, 1929

Hawaii seems to serve as an allegorical pot of gold at the end of a massive rainbow that apparently extends into the stratosphere on this 1934 magazine cover **(RIGHT)**, and Umi, the Hawaiian Boy Who Became a King glories in a more realistically-sized one in a 1928 children's book illustration by Robert Lee Eskridge **(BELOW)**.

"The sun, grand master of ceremonies, retired behind a curtain of sultry colors, leaving the scene set with towering trade clouds piled like white phantoms of temples . . ."

Hula Moons, 1930

Before color photography was perfected, tourists could buy gaudy postcards with artificially enhanced colors. The garish hues of these imagined "Hawaiian sunsets" (from the 1930's) are not permitted in nature!

Everywhere in the world, the moon is a symbol of love. It is even more so in Hawaii, where it serves to intensify an already romantic setting—or so it has been said. One who fell under its spell was poet and artist Don Blanding, an adventuresome native of Oklahoma who found his home state a little too humdrum to hang around in when there were lots more exciting places to be. Hawaii caught his fancy in 1916 when he saw a stage presentation of "The Bird of Paradise" and the exotic image it showed had him on a boat to the islands in a flash. Once arrived, he must have found things to his liking, for he soon was producing at a prolific rate. Blanding's sentimental verse and artwork were presented in a number of books from the 1920's through the 1950's, and although a wanderer by nature, Hawaii remained his favorite subject even when other locales charmed him away. Such was his attachment to Hawaii that he could claim co-credit for inventing Lei Day, a long-lived tradition of wearing leis on May 1st, in 1928. Shown here is the cover of Hula Moons **(TOP LEFT)**, which Blanding wrote in 1930, based on his experiences in Hawaii. The illustration is typical of his silhouette-filled style. Don Blanding wrote the words and theater organist Edwin Sawtelle the music for "There's Romance in the Moonlight of Hawaii" **(BELOW LEFT)**. The publication of this song coincided with the 1940 opening of the grand but ill-fated Hilo Theater, a structure that had the misfortune of being badly damaged by tidal waves twice (in 1946 and 1960) before being demolished in the early 1960's. **(FACING PAGE)**: a hula girl from a 1920's calendar revels in the pinkish glow of that fabulous Hawaiian moon.

"Hawaii nights! Hawaiian moon. And it's not a moon to be trifled with. It is potent. . . bewitching. . . (just to look is an adventure)."

Hawaii Tourist Bureau ad, 1931

Musically speaking, nothing in Hawaii has received quite the attention and praise that the moon has. Yes, you can see it from anywhere on earth, but isn't it more special here? Songwriters evidently think so. (FACING PAGE, LEFT TO RIGHT): sheet music featuring a boy and a girl and a field of very untropical poppies (1927), flying fishes having a nighttime romp (1939), and an abandoned hula girl with only the moon for company (1916). Below them, three record labels representing a wealth of songs recorded on the subject: (LEFT TO RIGHT), a 1950's disc by a still-popular performer, a 1937 tune from a Hollywood feature film, and another locally recorded effort from 1947. The "49th State" label (FAR LEFT) reflects the hopeful period around 1950 when statehood was thought to be imminent. Hawaii actually became the 50th state nine years later.

A 1922 couple (RIGHT), enjoying all the fabled aspects of Hawaii they've heard so much about—Waikiki Beach, an ukulele, Diamond Head, and (of course) the moon.

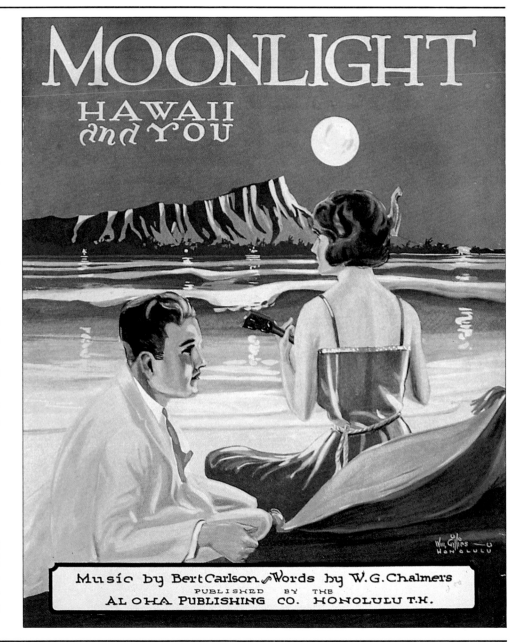

"You may see many beautiful pictures of the marvelously colored and shaped finny inhabitants of the deep, but until you see the things themselves you cannot realize their real beauty."

Hawaii by A Tourist, 1928

Just as colorful in their way as the flowers of Hawaii are the many exotic fish of the island waters. Not for the tropics are the dull greys and browns of temperate-zone fish, for here is a veritable swimming rainbow in the surf along a shoreline reef. For once, the descriptions aren't exaggerated. You can see for yourself what a delight Hawaii's multi-colored fish are in their natural habitat if you're adventuresome enough to do a little investigating with mask and snorkel. It has to be admitted, though, that you also must find a fairly unspoiled location to do your observing, since much aquatic life has been diminished by man's presence. An aquarium might have to serve instead.

Practically speaking, a lot of this riot of color is edible. Hawaiians spent much time in catching these same picturesque fish since they relied a great deal on the sea to feed themselves. In that case the eyecatching colors and shapes were clues to what was good to eat and what should be avoided.

If you weren't interested in eating any of these creatures or getting wet to look at them, you could still see them in a variety of other places. That's because under-water scenes of tropical fish and sinuous seaweed were a popular design in modernistic decorative schemes all over the world in the 1920's and 30's. No wonder you saw the same type of motifs used liberally in Hawaii in those years and later—since that's where the fish actually came from.

(FACING PAGE): "Fishes of Hawaii" postcard brochure, 1920's.

A favorite of artists portraying life beneath the sea was the "Moorish Idol" - an odd name for a fish the Hawaiians called kihikihi. Smartly attired in black, yellow, and white, these fellows were often seen as decoration in a number of situations. **(BELOW)**, a design from Kimo (1928), and **(RIGHT)**, the top of a Ta-Ro-Co Taro Cookie tin, from about 1930. (Taro is the source of Hawaii's famous paste-like dish, poi. Little wonder the cookies weren't a big hit).

". . . gaudy fishes flashing like spilled jewels among the coral and sand."

Colorful Hawaii, 1945

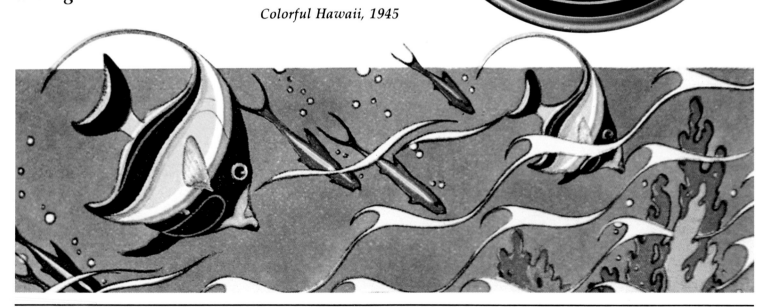

Kihikihi and shells float about on cloth from about 1950, **(RIGHT)**. The designer took some liberties in utilizing the coral plant in the background, so named because of the resemblance of its flower clusters to coral. In reality, it is strictly a land plant and would never be seen with fish swimming amongst its leaves.

More finny friends: fabric designs in particular made great use of fish and general underwater themes, especially in the postwar and early 50's era of loud aloha shirts. Here a few fish lazily make their way through coral and suggestions of watery movement **(LEFT)**. **(FACING PAGE):** a vertical motif from a 1948 luncheon menu from the S.S. President Monroe ("en route to Hawaii") with the usual assortment of undersea creatures and plant growth **(FAR RIGHT)**, and a postcard from the early 1900's showing a "Kanaka's Delight": fish and poi, naturally **(RIGHT)**.

*". . . the most marvelous sight . . . blue, green, saffron, garnet,
in families, in battalions the enchanting creatures went by. . ."*

Hawaii: Isles of Dreams, 1957

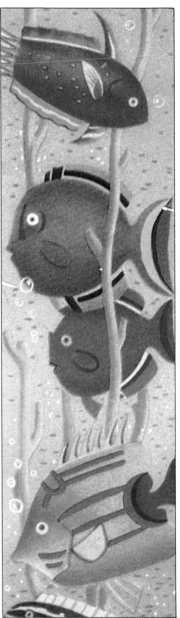

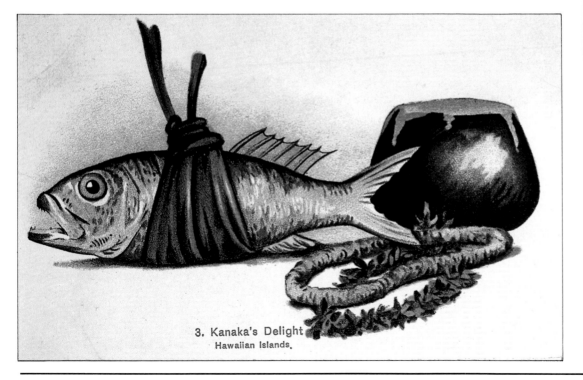

3. Kanaka's Delight
Hawaiian Islands.

"One can know the full deliciousness of Hawaiian pine-apple only by tasting it in Hawaii, picked in the day of its full ripeness when it is truly champagne-and-honey."

Colorful Hawaii, 1945

Bountiful **nature** gives to Hawaii a brimming cornucopia of fruits and flowers. The latter are a lovely accessory, a sort of ornamentation to life in paradise, while fruits are important economically. And, despite the tourist's perennial dream of being an idle island castaway, feeding himself by just reaching out to pluck a meal from the nearest tree, life is not that easy in Hawaii. Our food plants are fussed over just as much as they are in other parts of the world. More tender foodstuffs, or those produced only in small amounts, usually are sold locally. But for the ones that are exported considerable promotion is needed to convince people far across the sea that they really want "a taste of Hawaii". Sugar, Hawaii's largest cash crop, pretty much sells itself as a staple item, but the need for pineapples (number two in rank) has had to be implanted in Mrs. Average Housewife's consciousness. Fortunately, pineapples can benefit in advertising from being associated with Hawaii. "You have noticed that since 1908 the Hawaiian pineapple industry has not hid its light under a bushel but through cooperative advertising has made its market and yours bigger and bigger", stated a 1927 promotional booklet, pointing out how pineapple advertising was good for all business in Hawaii. And, in turn, the more Hawaii was known, the better it was for pineapples as well - would the fruit be as desirable if it came from the midwest, for example? Partly because of advertising, then, pineapple growing came to be an important industry in Hawaii.

Most people probably think of Hawaii as a land bursting with tropical blooms. It is, but many of the flowers that seem so typical of the islands are, like many of the people, immigrants from abroad. Sad to say, this influx of showy and aggressive plants brought in by human beings in a steady stream since the earliest Polynesians has crowded aside much of Hawaii's own unique flora. Ecological considerations notwithstanding, many of these foreign flowers have become beloved in Hawaii because of their beauty and fragrance, and are thought of as natives in the minds of many - enabling them to be used as suitable symbols of paradise.

(FACING PAGE): Savoy brand pineapple juice label, c. 1930.

FROM THE TROPICS
TO YOUR TABLE

Eighty-three

Tested Banana Recipes

Coconut

sun-sweetness from the tropics

Franklin Baker Company, *Inc.*
Hoboken, New Jersey

From the tropics to your table: eighty-three yummy things to do with bananas in this 1920's promotional recipe book (FACING PAGE, ABOVE), and a fabric design from around 1950, featuring (BELOW) "broad-leaved banana plants, sometimes with the bananas themselves hanging upside down in that queer way they have of doing" (The Polynesian magazine, 1934).

Another giveaway booklet to urge the use of coconuts in the home, available, like the banana one, by mail in the 1920's (ABOVE). (RIGHT), attention, class - a girl enjoys a coconut fresh off the tree at Waikiki as an illustration for "The Coconut", a "reading song" for children, from the local edition of The Music Hour, a 1929 school textbook.

The Hawaiian Pineapple Growers Association was never one to miss a publicity trick, from cannery tours to promotional photographs. Here's one **(RIGHT)** - we grow 'em BIG in the islands! Actually, though, "this huge steel pineapple towering above the Hawaiian Pineapple Company holds 100,000 gallons of water required for the sprinkling system" (not juice, as Honolulu folklore has long maintained). In the foreground crouches a cannery tour guide waiting to take you through the modern industrial complex.

(FACING PAGE, ABOVE): "Beauty Smothered with Beauty" is the title of this masterpiece, in which a blonde grits her teeth and smiles gamely from within a heap of heavy prickly pineapples. **(BELOW)**, a local variation of a form of postcard popular throughout the country during the first several decades of this century: the giant item. Depending on where the card was from, the big item could be anything from a peach to a grasshopper; in Hawaii, naturally, it was a pineapple. Here the fantasy fruit is plunked down in a pasture amidst some inquisitive cows while a native climbs up it as he would a coconut palm.

Fun with fruit: The pineapple princess **(ABOVE)** is from 1939 and is hereby honored for bravery for enduring this set-up. This pineapple **(RIGHT)** could probably feed a whole city (if it came to that) and dates from the early 1930's.

Regular print advertising was not neglected by the pineapple growers. Both of the ads shown here stress pineapple's connection to the charming land it's grown in, where it's packaged at the peak of perfection, then rushed to your favorite grocer. Two things to notice here: first, no specific brand is mentioned (these are promoting the industry as a whole), and second, only <u>canned</u> fruit is featured. That's because transportation was too slow at that time to allow fresh pineapples to make the lengthy trip to mainland markets without spoiling.

In this 1931 ad (FACING PAGE), two vertical motifs show the entire sweep of life in paradise, from fish bubbling underwater to lofty mountain peaks, that surrounds the pampered pineapple in its fields. (RIGHT): a ship speeds its precious cargo away from the rainbow-arched island where the huge symbolic "Any Brand" can reigns supreme, while below a thrilled maiden embraces a spiny patch of pineapple plants - all this from 1929.

Royal Hawaiian

ON THE BEACH AT WAIKIKI

"There are few places indeed, in the islands, where flowers of some sort are not in sight. Mostly, of course, these are the Hibiscus. . ."

Hawaiian Flowers, 1943

Not only fruits of many kinds grow in Hawaii, but countless flowers thrive too. One particularly floriferous inhabitant of the islands is Hawaii's state flower, the hibiscus. A pair of its blossoms adorns this page **(TOP)** from a 1956 Royal Hawaiian Hotel menu motif painted by Lloyd Sexton. The

hibiscus was especially popular in the 1920's, when local plant fanciers tried to outdo each other in breeding spectacularly colored and shaped blossoms. Later, these often turned up in fabric designs in fanciful and occasionally lurid colors.

Floral fantasy: huge jungle flowers surround the title character of <u>Kimo</u> (1928), drawn by Lucille Webster Holling **(RIGHT)**, while on the cover of the 1937 sheet music for "My Flow'r of Paradise" **(ABOVE RIGHT)**, a lady seems to be swooning over the romance of a leafy setting in a Hawaiian night.

"... dizzying combinations of floral colorings throughout the year, reaching a delirious crest in May and June when a tidal wave of flower-petals inundates the land."

Colorful Hawaii, 1945

Queen of the night: the romanticist's favorite flower has always been the night-blooming cereus. Not colorful or sweetly-scented, it still has a place in the hearts of poets and artists, who have practically shouldered each other aside in the rush to praise it. At first appearance it seems unworthy of this attention, for it's an undistinguished-looking plant; a spiny, snaky cactus that sits dully for most of the year, presenting little to interest the passer-by. But on occasional summer nights, the plant produces great numbers of giant white flowers with delicate stamen-filled centers. Should the moon happen to be shining down upon this marvelous display, well . . . even the most blase viewer can get a bit carried away. The contrast between the astonishing flowers and the rather unattractive plant on which they grow, and the fact that the blossoms last for only one night, make the night-blooming cereus fascinating to almost everyone.

A well-dressed lady (RIGHT) has arisen early to pick some of the fast-wilting flowers before the sun can ruin them. The scene is Punahou School's famous night-blooming cereus hedge, shown on an early 1900's postcard.

"But the most ethereal of all the island flowers is the delicate moon-worshipping cereus, which blooms only at night."

Nearby Hawaii, 1934

Night Blooming Cereus, Hawaii.

A song to honor the nocturnal flower (ABOVE), from 1936; and two dreamy lasses pay homage to a gigantic stylized night-blooming cereus **(RIGHT)** on one of the well-known Matson Line menus created by Frank MacIntosh in the late 1930's.

The Culture

L et's go native ...or something sort of like it! Presented in this chapter are the popular-culture versions of Hawaiian customs, sports, and traditions that seemed to be picturesque or interesting enough to warrant promotion as part of what Hawaii was supposed to be. Keep in mind that what's shown here is considerably more tidy and cheerful than reality ever was, and that even forty or fifty years ago island people were not living completely in "the old Hawaiian way". "Look where you will, you won't find Hawaiian girls bare to the waist or even merely draped in wreaths of flowers—unless you hire some to go out and pose for such pictures", said one travel writer in 1937. But in spite of such voices of reason, it was probably something of a shock for some people to arrive in Hawaii and find an American community complete with cars and telephones and plumbing, when they expected to see grass skirts and grass shacks. They expected these things, of course, because of the advertising they had seen that featured a "Hawaiian" way of life that never really existed.

Unfortunately, the "Hawaiian" activities that so many tourists have been seeing for decades now are, in many cases, sadly lacking in the original meanings that made them living traditions. The loss of the need to maintain certain practices of native life - such as fishing and canoeing - has turned those things into mere entertainment; little more than empty actions, put on for show. Such a condition is hardly unique to Hawaii; it's true all over the world now. Yet, ironically, the tourism that, on one hand, has served to undermine true Hawaiian traditions has also assisted in preserving them as a part of Hawaii's distinctiveness. By wanting to see the hula performed or to go surfing, tourists have awakened Hawaiians to the need to preserve these remnants of their culture before they are lost forever.

(FACING PAGE): Detail of a Matson Lines menu by Eugene Savage, late 1940's.

very racial group has its stereotypes and the Hawaiian people are no exception. For example: the men are large and love to play music, the women are hospitable and love to dance, and everyone can swim like fishes, which is what they do when they're not eating or sleeping. Nobody likes to work because life is so easy in paradise that strenuous exertion really isn't necessary.

It's obvious that all these cheerful clichés just aren't the whole truth. The Hawaiians never lived a totally carefree, idle life, particularly in the days before outside civilization arrived. Living off the land as they did was hard work, despite the romantic notions attached to this noble ideal. It's not that they didn't have time for fun, but they <u>did</u> have a lot to keep busy with.

Whether or not most people believed the "Happy Hawaiian" image is open to conjecture, but it certainly has been seen enough to make it completely familiar. This fabric design **(RIGHT)** contains all the important elements: the laughing ukulele player, the beautiful girl with the shy demeanor, the lazy fellow snoozing in the shade of a coconut palm, and the bountiful food all natives enjoy.

If the average American can be said to have any knowledge of what the Hawaiian language sounds like, it would mostly be due to popular music. Hawaiian theme'd songs have achieved mass acceptance in two main phases, which differed greatly in their authenticity of language. The first phase, inspired by the success of the 1912 Broadway production of "The Bird of Paradise", peaked around 1916 and was characterized by the use of an often silly parody of the Hawaiian tongue that still persists. For example: "Oh, How She Could Yacki Hacki Wicki Wacki Woo (That's Love In Honolu)". . . need we say more? That may be "love in Honolu" but it's sure not the way they talk there! Hawaiian music's next appearance in the public's awareness came in the 1930's, spurred by national radio shows. This time there was authentic Hawaiian incorporated into melodies by people who were really familiar with the language—a far cry from the situation 20 years before, when the average Tin Pan Alley tunesmith knew only three key words to be used in every "island love-song": "Honolulu", "hula", and "Waikiki".

Tryin' to speak Hawaiian: "Yaaka Hula Hickey Dula" **(RIGHT)** really started the imitation-Hawaiian gibberish in 1916 that is still some people's idea of how the language sounds. Two Johnny Noble compositions **(ABOVE)** from 1935 and '36 serve as a comment on the later craze that was far more legitimate-sounding.

One of Hawaii's contributions to popular music, and certainly a favorite subject for artists, was the ukulele. Of Portuguese origin, it was introduced to the islands by immigrants from that country in the 1880's. The instrument became known to the rest of the U.S.A. by means of the many Hawaiian entertainers who played vaudeville houses and county fairs in the first decades of this century, and especially at the 1915 San Francisco Pan-Pacific Exposition. The Hawaiian music boom that got underway then helped further the ukulele's fame. The uke's small size made it the perfect accessory for the "flaming youth" of the 1920's, and the "collegiate" fellow strumming away became a cliché of the decade. After this craze peaked the ukulele's use tapered off; except in Hawaii, where it continues to be a favorite both for children and adults.

The ukulele is so integral to Hawaiian music that it seems like a native. These ukes all tangled up in leis are from song folios dating from 1934 **(FACING PAGE, ABOVE)** and 1944 **(ABOVE)**, while the Frank MacIntosh Matson menu is from the late 1930's **(RIGHT)**. The 1950's "Musical Hawaii" fabric **(FACING PAGE, BELOW)** deletes the leis and pictures an ukulele with authentic Hawaiian instruments.

As we've already seen, one popular idea about the Hawaiian people is that they love to eat. With that in mind, you can assume that mealtimes would be special—and they were, when the occasion was special enough to warrant having a luau.

The main attraction of this feast has always been the kalua pig, featured here in these depictions. Its preparation is elaborate. First a large hole is dug and lined with leaves, then the pig is placed in it and, in turn, is itself filled with heated stones. The whole thing is then buried for several hours to cook. At the appointed time, all gather round to unearth the main course and get down to some serious eating. Why all this just to cook some pork? It's easy to see the process as just another picturesque custom, but the Hawaiians didn't do it to be unusual—they had no other way, lacking metal utensils and large ovens. Cooking a pig in an imu is a tradition that has survived beyond its age of necessity as not only a tourist function but also as a cultural link to the past.

You're at a luau now: lavish food and good fellowship is offered to all at these native feasts, two of which are illustrated on the covers of the famous Matson Lines cruise ship menus. **(FACING PAGE)**: these exuberant merrymakers certainly have lots to eat in this typically abundant array painted by Eugene Savage, whose work was used by Matson in the postwar period. The style of his predecessor Frank MacIntosh **(RIGHT)** suggests a more refined group of diners. The rainbow-like glow surrounding the food can be attributed to artistic license, not radiation! **(BELOW)**, a more down-to-earth scene from <u>Kimo</u> (1928).

This luau (LEFT), pictured on a late 1940's postcard, isn't just an ordinary occasion. That's because these partygoers are enjoying delicious chilled Dole Pineapple Juice with their fish and poi. And speaking of poi, does it really taste like "library paste", as the cliché goes? Well, who knows? Who's ever eaten enough library paste to be able to compare the two? Regardless of whatever poi tastes like, every visitor has to try at least a finger or two just to be able to say he's done it.

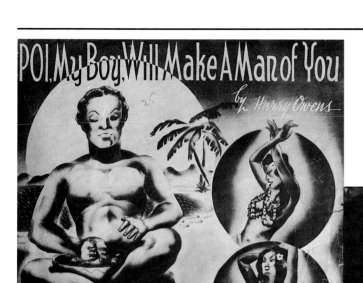

"The 'luau'... served with all the trimmings... pink salt, queer fish dishes, fresh coconut, and of course poi."

The Story of Hawaii, c. 1930

"Poi, My Boy, Will Make A Man Of You" (ABOVE, from 1940) thinks Gracie Allen as she feeds some to hubby George Burns in the late 1930's (RIGHT).

"Yes, they still dance the hula—that sunshine gesture of olden days—in Honolulu."

A Picture Trip to Hawaii, 1926

The embodiment of Hawaii has forever been, and probably forever will be, a beautiful woman clad in native dress. She turns up in all sorts of places for all sorts of reasons. She offers a lei or plays the ukulele or dances the hula or pulls in a fishing net; she pours beer or ginger ale or pineapple juice and hopes you'll try some: she sweeps with a new broom to add a touch of glamor to the otherwise prosaic world of housekeeping; or when all that gets too tiring, she simply lazes among the palms and gazes longingly out to sea. She is charming and alluring and always hospitable, especially to any Caucasian man.

This could be said to be the story behind the Hawaiian female who seems to have graced the presence of every aspect of Hawaiian commercial art. She is, in fact, a more exotic version of the ideal woman envisioned in American popular culture for decades.

Was the woman of Hawaii ever really like this? Well, to begin with, she never wore the costume you're used to seeing her in just to live her daily life. At no time in history could you have strolled down the beach and seen a woman strumming an ukulele unless she was having her picture taken. She first appeared in her now-traditional outfit in the early 1900's, and by then her grass skirt had been around as an import from other areas of the Pacific for about 20 years. By the 1920's, it was shortened to a fashionable knee-length; a decade later her skirt might be made of deeply-colored cellophane for a splash of swankiness, joining her already synthetic paper (and later - gasp! - plastic) lei. She can, of course, appear in modern streetclothes, but it is in her hula garb that we know her best.

She is totally the creation of commercialism and popular culture. She sums up, in one attractive package, what Hawaii can offer. Her commercial application does not diminish her good-natured acceptance as Hawaii's instantly recognizable image. Throughout it all she has remained cheerful and welcoming, which is, after all, her function.

(FACING PAGE): The Hawaiian Hula booklet, 1944.

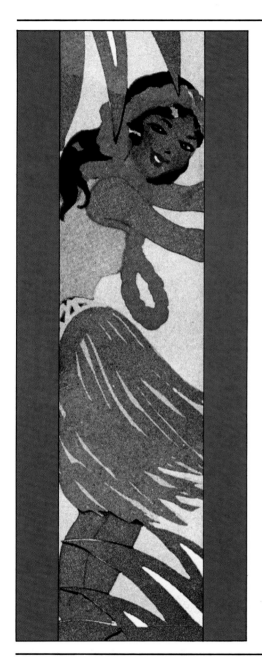

That funny South Sea dance: there are hula dancers both serious and sensuous, cheerful and carefree. The lady on the cover of "Do The Hula" **(RIGHT)** seems to know some rather unconventional movements. Her bare-breastedness is also rather unconventional for 1936, but as usual a handy flower lei keeps her within the limits of propriety. Besides, being from another culture, she's allowed to bend the rules a bit. More familiar is the pose of the simply-drawn girl **(LEFT)** who serves as a colorful motif in The Story of Hawaii, a fairly extensive and ornately written promotional booklet published by the Hawaii Tourist Bureau around 1930 and made available by mail. (The same title was used for other editions of similar pieces of literature put out by the Bureau for several years.)

(FACING PAGE): two groups of hula dancers display a degree of synchronization beyond the capacity of real human beings: **(FAR RIGHT)**, a slightly malevolent-looking trio gestures in a detail from a fresco painted by artist and sculptor Marguerite Blasingame in the foyer of the original Waikiki Theater in 1936; and **(NEAR RIGHT)**, a happy quartet forms a sarong sorority in one of the Matson Lines' menus painted by Eugene Savage between 1938 and 1940. Executed

first as six 4-by-8 foot murals, these works were not used commercially by Matson until about seven years after their completion. By 1951 more than 125,000 copies of the menus bearing these designs had been given away to ship passengers or sold at a small cost, and they had also been selected to become a permanent part of the collection of the Smithsonian Institute.

"Thus was born the hula . . . the dream of a goddess, translated into the poetry of movement."

Hawaii U.S.A., 1942

If our Hawaiian lady wasn't dancing the hula, then at least she ought to have been clutching an ukulele to show her musical tastes. In fact, the ukulele was almost a required accessory to go with the grass skirt and lei, and many a pretty gal put on all three and was thus transformed into a "real Hawaiian". It was through representations like these that the popular idea of the standardized hula girl was established all over the world.

Four versions of the ukulele dream girl; (THIS PAGE), a small 1930's pin-up in a provocative but friendly pose; and (FACING PAGE), the original "Ukulele Lady" (1925) and two of her sisters from the same decade - a maiden longing for ice cream in a Maxfield Parrish-like setting on a metal advertising tray, and a calendar girl who, although topless, seems warm enough in the glow of an apparent campfire.

> "Yes, travellers see the hula
> every other place they go—
> So we dance it here, a little,
> to be up-to-date, you know!"
>
> *Paradise of the Pacific, 1924*

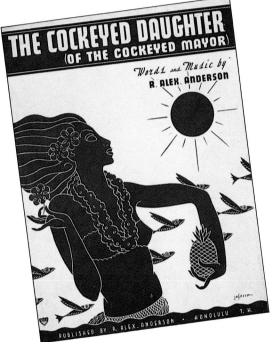

These three very stylish ladies represent the outstanding work of an artist identified only as "LaSalle" who designed dozens of tasteful and distinctive locally-printed sheet music covers between 1934 and 1941. **(FACING PAGE),** a dainty girl dreamily pulls in a fishing net - one of the famous Frank Mac-Intosh Matson menus from the 1930's.

The lovely Hawaiian maid manages to turn up just about anywhere, and she's usually helping to sell something. These pages give an idea of how far the commercial use of a pretty girl has gone, but they're only just a hint. We could go on for pages more!

Below are the "Bardell Miniatures": a packet of photos of two fairly sedate hula girls in discreet poses, dating from the 1920's. The big boom in this sort of thing occurred later, during World War II, but the wartime pinups were often less restrained. Such snapshots might have been the closest that many of the servicemen who passed through Hawaii in those years ever got to anything like a hula girl. In the middle of the page is the Clean Sweep lady, thoughtfully churning up a cloud of dust with her vigorous sweeping, which goes to show that even in paradise the floor can get dirty. This was not the only product label that featured a hula girl - you could also spot her on soda pop bottles, macadamia nut cans, and even butter wrappers (along with a friendly cow). In the upper corner of this page repose the Hula Girl playing cards from the late 1920's, which bear a romantic motif that would allow weary card players a chance to drift off with thoughts of a native maiden in the moonlight.

HONOLULU BROOM FACTORY

Clean Sweep

Hula gals: 1920's souvenir photos **(FAR LEFT)**, 1950's broom label **(NEAR LEFT)**, and playing cards from the 1920's **(ABOVE)**.

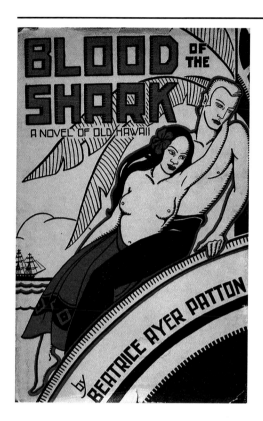

A torrid-looking couple (the typical Caucasian male/Hawaiian female pairing) adorns the cover of the 1936 novel Blood of the Shark, above. The author, Beatrice Ayer Patton, was a sweet little old lady who happened to have been the wife of World War II's famous General George Patton, and it was while they were stationed in Hawaii that she penned the work. In a less physical encounter, a helpful native girl pours some Hawaiian Dry Pale Ginger Ale for a sailor and engenders goodwill between military and civilian in a 1925 newspaper ad (center). The drawing is by John Kelly, well-known in Hawaii in later years for his etchings of beautiful island women. The sly Hawaiian lass in the bottom corner of this page (from the cover of the 1935 Paradise of the Pacific magazine Holiday Number) looks as if she's ready to give a special welcome to a passenger she's spied disembarking from the Lurline. If she's like her sisters shown here she won't waste any time getting to know him.

More hula gals: 1936 book cover (ABOVE), 1925 newspaper ad (NEAR RIGHT), and 1935 magazine cover (FAR RIGHT).

Hawaiian eyes are full of pep and ginger;
They have the tropic charm--they make you sigh;
They sparkle like the moonlight on the water;
They're just exactly like HAWAIIAN DRY.

HAWAIIAN DRY
PALE
Ginger Ale

"Happy days on peacock-blue water are enjoyed at Waikiki . . . with a good surf running, you will be dashed shoreward at 25 or 30 miles an hour."

A Picture Tour of the Hawaiian Islands, c. 1930

Surrounded completely by the ocean, Hawaii is naturally a center for water-related activities. Canoes cut through the sea in long-distance races, while at any beach, surfboards of all shapes and sizes crowd the waves. These two pastimes of the ancient Hawaiians have spread to other parts of the world in varying degrees, but they remain strongest in the land where they originated.

The Hawaiians developed their seagoing skills from living in close connection with the ocean both for recreation and by necessity. This was a major source of food for them, as is well known, but in Hawaii's wonderful climate it could also be enjoyed just for pleasure at any time of the year. Generations of attention to how the sea behaved and how it could be used safely gave the Hawaiians knowledge that became a part of their culture.

Watching a surfer today, or taking an outrigger canoe ride just for the fun of it, you might not think that these "sports" were important in the olden days. That's because we've lost much of the knowledge that once was integral to surfing and canoeing. We view them now simply as picturesque aspects of the islands that anyone can enjoy, but those who really know the background to these two sports realize that more than just physical action is involved. For them, these activities are a way of continuing a tradition that is important to preserve, not only for the Hawaiian culture but also as a way to retain an appreciation and respect for the sea.

In the end, though, it's not necessary to know the deeper meaning to see that both surfing and canoeing function as symbols of healthy outdoor living in Hawaii—even for those living miles away who might never even have seen the ocean.

(FACING PAGE): paper sticker with surfing motif, early 1940's.

B y the 20th century the Hawaiian canoe was no longer essential to families depending on the sea for food, for newer and faster kinds of boats superceded the outrigger canoe as a fisherman's craft. But happily, some sensible people continued to use it for sport and for fun. And the processes of westernization that threatened it also provided a reason for its survival: tourism. Many of the canoes still in existence in the early decades of this century were in use at Waikiki, where visitors could be taken for a quick thrilling ride on the usually docile surf — which didn't seem all that small once you got in it!

This Hawaiian couple (LEFT) might be employed in some tourist-related field, posing with the lei-adorned prow of a canoe named "Aloha" pulled up on the silver sands of Waikiki. They are the creation of local artist John Kelly, and were originally seen on the back cover of the Hawaii Tourist Bureau's 1929 edition of The Story of Hawaii.

A suggestion of olden days as an aged canoemaker tests out a newly-built craft with the help of some young friends **(LEFT)**, in Robert Lee Eskridge's <u>Umi</u> (1936). **(BELOW)**, a more modern scene of canoeing fun from a 1929 <u>Paradise of the Pacific</u> magazine.

"A pause before the final lunge. Suddenly, your face is cutting the salt wind! Prow and outrigger hurl an avalanche of spray overhead."

Hawaii, U.S.A., 1942

Hawaiian beachboys were a well-known feature of Waikiki, serving as sort of unofficial lifeguards and social directors for surfside activities. One of several songs praising these "modern sons of Neptune" is this 1938 example **(ABOVE)**. Little Shirley Temple is made an honorary captain in the Waikiki Beach Patrol in 1935, while on one of the visits she made to Hawaii during her days of stardom **(RIGHT)**.

"**What Are The Wild Waves Say-ing**" is the musical question asked **(BELOW)**, from 1937, as a happy group takes off on an exciting ride towards shore. These folks **(RIGHT)** (on the cover of a 1936 photobook) are just setting out for their fun with the helpful beachboys getting them underway.

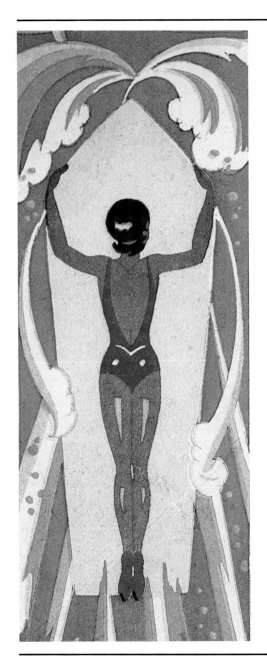

Surfing is easily Hawaii's best-known and most widespread sport. There's no telling why the ancient Hawaiians first started surfing, or exactly when, but the activity was well established in the culture by the time the first westerners arrived in the late 1700's. As with so many things, to the Hawaiians, surfing had meanings beyond the simple riding of waves. Their closeness to nature, and their respect and awareness of it, meant that they imparted a significance to surfing beyond what people attach to it today. And, in the same way that their daily lives were regulated, the ancient Hawaiians were under restrictions as to who could surf where, and with what kind of surfboard.

With the decline of Hawaiian civilization and the arrival of westerners, came the interconnected decline of surfing. Not only was the practice frowned upon by the new rulers of the islands, but the actual Hawaiian population itself dropped disastrously, meaning that there were fewer people surfing. By the early 1900's the sport was almost dead, until the first steps to revive it were taken at Waikiki. Folklore said that only at Waikiki were conditions acceptable for surfing—it was "the one place in the world where the contour of the ocean bottom and the protecting coral reef combine to supply the right kind of continuous surf crests for the sport", according to a 1930 source. Of course, as time passed, this was proven wrong as surfing spread to other areas in Hawaii as well as other parts of the world, notably California and Australia, beginning in the 1930's. The big boom really didn't come until new lighter and more maneuverable surfboards started to be developed in the 1950's; by the next decade surfing achieved the status of a national fad and became a sport firmly entrenched in the mind of the country and the world.

Skimming the silver surf: two Hawaiian fellows ride the waves, undoubtedly at Waikiki, on these two items from the 1920's **(FACING PAGE)** - a guidebook **(FAR RIGHT)** and a postcard booklet **(NEAR RIGHT)**. On this page **(LEFT)**, a bird's eye view of a girl lying flat on her surfboard as she catches a wave; a design from The Story of Hawaii, from 1930.

"The surf-riders are often called 'Gods of the Seas' . . . because as they ride the stampeding white-maned stallions of the surf they seem to be flying . . . "

Colorful Hawaii, 1945

Where the surfboard speeds: forty or fifty years ago, surfing was still strongly identified with Hawaii, because hardly anyone did it anywhere else. The use of a surfing motif, as shown here, could only be a reference to Hawaii. **(LEFT)**: wiping out is no fun for these two Hawaiian lads from <u>Kimo</u> (1928); a vibrant scene with jazzed-up colors by artist Lucille Webster Holling. **(FACING PAGE)**: Al Kealoha Perry and his backup group manage to sing and surf at the same time according to this 1950 label off a 78rpm record **(NEAR RIGHT)**, and the one and only Duke Kahanamoku in his early days pokes his board out of the frame of a 1914 promotional postcard and makes it all look so effortless **(FAR RIGHT)**.

"Standing on a comet in a spray of blue and gold and diamonds. That's surf-board riding at Waikiki!"

See All of Hawaii, c. 1925

Fishing is an engaging subject for artists and an interesting process to observe, but for the Hawaiians it was the mainstay of their existence. The islands' waters hold many forms of edible aquatic life, often conveniently close to shore. This was fortunate for the first inhabitants of Hawaii, since there are places where it would be difficult to live at all were it not for the abundance of the sea.

Two main methods were used. The pictures on this page demonstrate throw-netting, which really is an art that must be learned. "Few statues could be more dramatic and beautiful than a bronze Hawaiian fisherman, standing on a rock in the foaming waters, peering with trained eyes into the depths, waiting to hurl the circular net . . ." said one writer in 1940. Once hurled, the net has (it's hoped) trapped a number of fishes underneath; after that comes the process of disentangling it from the rocks it is now firmly clinging to. Repairs are frequent, but throw-netting is a very productive method of fishing, once the technique is learned.

On the facing page is a hukilau, where large nets are laid from canoes offshore and are eventually pulled up onto the beach by a happy throng. Popular culture has turned the hukilau into a sort of fun-for-everyone type of occasion, primarily due to a well-known song on the subject and the simple hula that goes with it, which every begining hula student invariably learns.

Gone fishin': throw-netters and nighttime spearfishermen are surrounded by examples of the undersea life they are searching for in this fabric design **(FAR LEFT)**, while Kimo **(BELOW)** will certainly find lots to catch with his throw-net (from Kimo, 1928). **(FACING PAGE)**: exuberant natives bring in their bountiful hukilau haul on the cover of a late 1940's Matson Lines menu by Eugene Savage.

"The custom of stringing these colorful and fragrant flowers into garlands makes one of Hawaii's most dearly loved rituals."

Colorful Hawaii, 1945

The Hawaiian people, living so close to nature, indulged the human tendency to self-ornamentation by wearing leis. They developed the making of these wreaths of flowers, leaves, and other materials far more than did other peoples of the Pacific. Leis were important to the Hawaiians and have retained their importance even today.

For most people, the custom of giving leis is especially connected with travelling. In the past, when tourists came to the islands in rather small and manageable numbers, just about everyone could expect a flowery wreath or two to be hung around their neck as they got off their ship, for even if no one was meeting them, some determined islanders made sure they wouldn't be missed by this pleasant greeting. The lei sellers could be found in downtown Honolulu then, near enough to the docks to be present when they were needed. You could also purchase a lei from the many vendors who operated from decrepit autos and trucks parked in Waikiki. Later, as the pace picked up, lei sellers vanished from their informal sidewalk locations to appear in well-organized airport stands.

The wearing of leis has long been associated with important occasions as well. Visiting politicians and movie stars were inevitably photographed wearing leis, and every so often one or two of these garlands will turn up far away from Hawaii at things like political conventions, presented by some island resident.

Many Hawaiian customs have disappeared, but the giving of leis continues to thrive. Not only are they still common in Hawaii; they've come to be yet another easily recognized bit of Hawaiiana that has entered the world of popular culture - another symbol of Hawaii.

(FACING PAGE): "My Lei of Leis" sheet music, 1937.

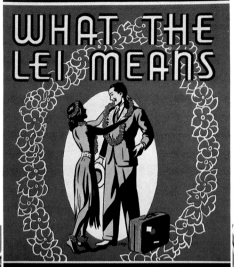

Most people who aren't from the islands would probably consider leis to be adornments for women only. Actually both sexes wear leis pretty equally in Hawaii, but he-men from across the sea can be excused for being a little hesitant to sport a bunch of flowers. **(RIGHT)**, the fellow on the cover of the sheet music for "What The Lei Means", from 1936, seems to be so taken by the (apparently) topless hula girl who's making the pres-

entation that he doesn't mind. In this fabric design **(BELOW)** a similar lei girl glories in the many garlands she's all wrapped up in. She is a close copy of the Matson Line women created by Fred MacIntosh (see page 63, for example); such cribbing of motifs from other sources is typical of Hawaiian fabrics, as are the sort of strange color combinations used here, which give the girl what looks like blue lipstick.

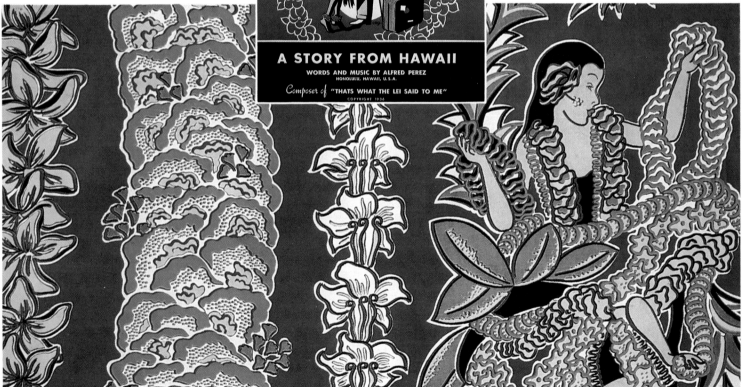

"The average price—you may gasp if you like—is twenty-five cents, and this will mean, for instance, a chain of one hundred ginger blossoms."

Hawaii with Sydney A. Clark, 1939

The well-dressed couple and pretty lei girl **(ABOVE)** are from a piece of sheet music from the mid-1930's; a real-life counterpart to this scene (from the same period) is this photo **(LEFT)** in which a pair of professional models bargain for leis at the Honolulu docks.

The Story of Hawaii

"No prettier or more touching custom may be witnessed any place than that of placing leis around the necks of arriving or departing friends."

Hawaii, Eternally Enchanting, 1924

KUU LEI
(My Wreath of Flowers)
W. Kolomoku

HT 220

Hawaiian Recording Quartet
Maika Hanapi

ADVERTISER PUBLISHING CO., LTD.
RECORDED IN HONOLULU, HAWAII

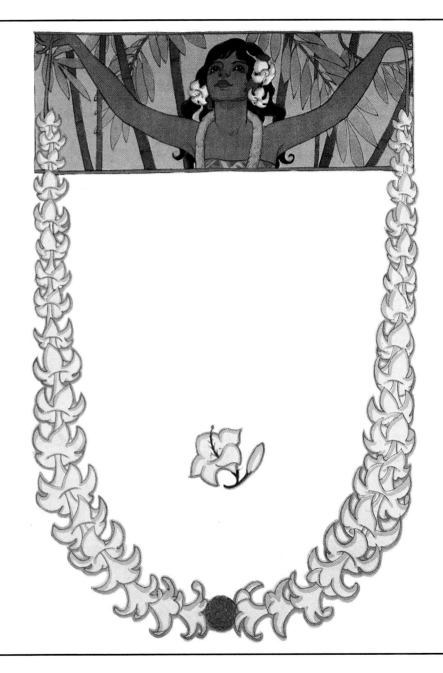

Lure of the lei: more happy lei girls, more pretty leis. **(FACING PAGE)**: this beaming vendor **(FAR LEFT)** appeared on the cover of The Story of Hawaii, from 1929. This rendering, by John Kelly, was one of two that were used extensively for promotional purposes around this time. Both were based on a photograph of a real person, who probably was a paid model instead of a real lei seller. **(NEAR LEFT)**: not terribly showy, but cherished nonetheless, are the intertwined maile and ilima leis that form a border motif on the label of Hawaii's first local record company, Hawaiian Transcription Productions. Founded in 1936, H.T.P. sold commercially-available discs like this one in addition to offering to record anyone at all for several dollars at the KGU radio studios - "with Hawaiian music in the background." **(RIGHT)**: Lani, the heroine of the 1928 children's book Kimo, stretches out a long lei she has strung.

The Visitor

T he fabric motif on the facing page sums up a welcome for what has become the most important economic force in Hawaii: the visitor. In this final chapter, we'll look at aspects of tourism in the isles—the transportation that people used to get here, the places they stayed in, the souvenirs they bought, and the promotional devices that convinced them to make the trip to begin with.

In the mid-20th century, Hawaii's economy underwent a fundamental change from one based upon agriculture to one relying on tourism. Not only did this change mean a great growth in service industries which took care of the needs of vacationers, but it also meant a change in the lives of Hawaii's workforce. Generally speaking, the sons and daughters of sugar and pineapple plantation workers grew up to be employed by hotels and tour companies.

In a larger context, the increasing reliance on tourism for a strong economy meant that Hawaii needed to be better known throughout the country and the world. Accordingly, the industries serving the visitor—the steamship companies and airlines, the hotels, and the makers of alohawear and souvenirs—all had to advertise themselves. The islands have been fortunate that, on the whole, the growth of their main activity has been a steady and healthy affair with few reverses. To keep things that way, however, it was important that the prospective traveller must always be aware that Hawaii awaited him, and that once he arrived all the comforts of home were available. Hawaii, too, turned increasingly to advertising itself, usually through the campaigns prepared by the Hawaii Visitors Bureau and its predecessors. Once the awareness of Hawaii was aroused in people's minds, indirect promotion could come from other sources, such as radio or the movies. All of these media have helped keep the islands topics of conversation. Sometimes, to be sure, the attractions have been overstated, but Hawaii always has had lots to offer. As long as that remains true, the pleasant memories of a Hawaiian vacation will continue to keep the visitors coming - as they have been coming for so long.

(FACING PAGE): detail of fabric, probably from the postwar years.

Nowadays, **ship travel** is a luxurious alternative, but before 1936, if you wanted to visit Hawaii you had to come by boat. It wasn't all that short a jaunt — 5 or 6 days one way, which meant that the total trip had to last at least 2 weeks just in transit. Starting from anywhere east of San Francisco or Los Angeles added days more as well. All this movement ended up costing a fair amount of dough and thus the average tourist tended to be pretty well-heeled, with not too tight a schedule to keep back home.

Catering to just such a class of people was the Matson Navigation Company. Although you could have hopped aboard any number of vessels steaming from coast to isles, most travellers came via Matson. Preeminent among the lines serving Hawaii, Matson fulfilled its role quite nicely by going after those with the time and money to travel in a tasteful and elegant manner. Their advertising featured the smart set at sea, in a way that made you wish you could join them. Not everyone could afford a $1200 suite (one way), but even if you were paying the $80 fare you could still enjoy some of the luxury that was being touted.

Helping to perpetuate this impression of sumptuousness were the marvelous graphic designs of

Frank MacIntosh, which first appeared in the late 1930's. He created a world where slim, langorous women lounged amidst stylized blossoms, epitomizing the dreamy Polynesian rapture that would drift over the visitor upon arrival. MacIntosh's unmistakable look appeared on all of Matson Lines' printed matter and managed to blend the 1930's moderne style with a Hawaiian theme to complete success. So responsive was the public to this work that his menus, in particular, were saved in quantity by shipgoers to serve as decoration for living room or bedroom. By 1941, this was so common that one writer mentioned how a "Mat-

son Line menu cover framed in bamboo gave every (home) its note of local color." There are homes even today that are graced by such artwork, which still manages to evoke the ideal dream of Hawaii even after more than 40 years.

The work of Frank MacIntosh can be seen throughout this book. Shown here are two pieces by him, left and far right. Later Matson advertising by other artists kept up the same high standards, as evidenced by the ocean liner at right, speeding across the cover of a passenger list.

Smooth sailing: Frank MacIntosh's airbrushed glamor was used for approximately 10 years by the Matson Lines, from the late 1930's to about 1947, but during some of this period the ships were serving military purposes and weren't carrying civilian passengers. The luggage sticker **(UPPER LEFT)** was printed in 1946; the ticket envelope **(FACING PAGE, FAR RIGHT)** is from 1939. Another artist produced the view of Matson's queen ship, the Lurline in 1950 **(RIGHT)**.

MATSON LINE

HONOLULU

HOW DO YOU DO!

Words and Music by
Philip F. Phelps

PUBLISHED BY
PAUL F. SUMMERS
ROYAL HAWAIIAN MUSIC SHOP
ROYAL HAWAIIAN HOTEL — HONOLULU T. H.

Honolulu how do you do: The arrival of one of the big ocean liners was always a grand event filled with excitement and fun. Those on shore could ride out on smaller boats to give an early greeting before the incoming ship docked, although not usually in quite the manner seen on this 1932 sheet music **(LEFT)**. Once on land, arriving passengers could promptly be smothered in leis like these worry-free travellers **(BELOW)**, from a 1930 advertisement.

We had all the fun
for Castle & Cooke took all the worries!

Despite this view **(RIGHT)** from a 1920's travel brochure, a large steamship never drew up alongside a nearly deserted coastline for a few curious natives to wave a casual greeting. The docking scene actually took place in bustling downtown Honolulu, with the tallest building in all of Hawaii standing guard above the proceedings: Aloha Tower, built in 1925, which soared to a dizzying height of 10 stories (seen **ABOVE**, quaintly wreathed in leis.) So congested did the downtown area become on "Boat Days," a 1938 newspaper editorial grumped, that you might find yourself being forced to park as far as 3 blocks away from the docks! Modern problems even in paradise.

Propellers over paradise: 1929 was a good year for those in Hawaii who hated being seasick but needed to travel between islands, for in that year Inter-Island Airways (now Hawaiian Air) first took off. Then, rather than being mercilessly tossed by the cruel sea, you could swiftly wing through the sky and hope that airsickness could be avoided instead. "Beneath Inter-Island Sikorsky Planes Flash A Thousand Scenes," trumpeted the ads.

Air travel between Hawaii and the mainland had to wait until 1935 and the thrilling arrival of Pan American Airways' China Clipper. The trip lasted a tiring 18 hours, but at $278 one way it was still comparable to first-class ship passage and you saved a considerable amount of time. When civilian air travel resumed after World War II it soon supplanted luxury liners forever.

Airplanes perhaps lack a bit of the romance of ships, but they look more dynamic. Here an intrepidly-piloted biplane arrives over an island coastline in the 1928 children's book Kimo (**RIGHT**).

Winging it: a 1934 Inter-Island Airways brochure for the flight-minded tourist **(LEFT)**, is backed by fabric featuring a United Airlines promotion called "Hiway to Hawaii". Garments made of this cloth were sold thoughout the country by J.C. Penney in 1951.

"A beach of dreams, guarded by an extinct volcano, is Waikiki, the heart of Hawaii's playground."

A Picture Tour of the Hawaiian Islands, c. 1930

Ah, that world-famed locale, "the beach at Waikiki." That, of course, is where movie stars vacationed on the golden sands and those sweet brown maidens danced the hula all day long and beachboys cavorted in the surf among the flying fish and swank hotels peeked from amid the palms. The water was warm and the sky above was always blue and couldn't we fall in love there, me and you?

Well, perhaps we could; but the scene at Waikiki, the most famous beach in the world, never was and never will be quite exactly like this. What is it really like? Waikiki is actually a narrowish beach which is no more scenic than many others, but somehow this place has come to suggest the glamor, fun, and excitement of the exotic tropics. So how did it achieve such fame? Through promotion and advertising, that's how. TV and radio entertainment came to you "live from the beach at Waikiki." On the screen you saw Bing Crosby and John Wayne and Jerry Lewis singing or sleuthing or taking pratfalls there. Newspapers pictured corporate presidents and debutantes and royalty relaxing on its famous sands. And if all of them were there, shouldn't you be too?

For the many who decided that yes, they ought to be there too, came a host of hotels and other subsidiary growths, and the Waikiki district became the clearinghouse for all tourist activities in Hawaii. In spite of the oft-voiced complaint that it's been "ruined", Waikiki has been and still is where the great majority of visitors head, and where a lot of them are content to spend their time in the islands.

Why have so many come to Waikiki? Probably because it has still managed to retain some of the fun and glamour that brought people to it in the first place, despite its somewhat money-hungry aura. Perhaps it was because those who have visited still had, in the back of their minds, a faint memory of the movie stars and sweet brown maidens and beachboys cavorting in the surf . . .

(FACING PAGE): "Along The Way To Waikiki" sheet music, 1917.

Waikiki, you're calling me: in the 1920's, ideas about outdoor activities changed dramatically. It became acceptable, especially for young people, to go outside and actually exert themselves without wearing yards of thick clothing. Bathing suits shrank and exposed more skin, which for the first time could become fashionably tanned. What better place to do this than at Waikiki? All the chic hotels were there, and besides, who'd want to come all the way out to Hawaii and stay at some downtown place that looked like Akron? A few old stick-in-the-muds did, but the sun-splashed beach was where the lively set gathered. Their antics inspired commercial artist Martin R. Aden, who specialized in light-hearted caricatures like these, to capture some impressions of a "mawvelous" frolicsome Jazz Age afternoon in 1929 **(LEFT)**.

"I can see the bright umbrellas on the beach, catch the scent of coconut oil, and feel the extraordinary warmth of the water, and hear the laughter of smart people from everywhere."

Hawaii, late 1930's

"Waikiki's fame is due to the fact that here originated the sport of surf riding. There is no other place where long distance surf riding is enjoyed."

All About Hawaii, 1928

Back in the 1920's, surfing was being revived after nearly becoming extinct, and it was happening at Waikiki. Many people thought that it wasn't even possible to surf anywhere else than on Waikiki's special waves. Even after that particular misconception was put to rest, Waikiki remained the center for water sports in Hawaii, and this fabric design from about 1950 celebrates these aquatic activities **(RIGHT).**

In the early part of the century, Waikiki was quite distinct from the main urban part of the city of Honolulu. It was agricultural, and though you could go ocean-bathing there - and a few people had beach homes - it was primarily marshy farmland where rice was grown, ducks paddled about, and mosquitos flourished.

An exception to this otherwise rural scene was the Moana Hotel. Built in 1901, it was a rather grand structure rising 5 stories above its scrubby surroundings, visible from all over the fairly unpopulated area that is now Honolulu. It faced a very wide but uncrowded street on the land side and boasted a long pier that jutted into the sea on the other. The pavilion at the end of this pier was a perfect spot to snap photos of beachboys clowning on their surfboards, and at night, to enjoy a romantic interlude. An immense banyan tree sheltered outdoor diners in the court of the hotel where you could also meet that special someone for a nighttime dance. The Moana was elegant in its day, and is still charming and certainly beloved.

In the 1920's, an immense dredging and landfill project dramatically transformed Waikiki. Out went the farms and the smelly waters that had covered the district. Now, in their place, was white coral chip acreage awaiting development. A far cry it still was, though, from today's highrise-choked area; for although dry land now existed decades would be needed for all of it to be built on. Instead, hotels were concentrated along the beach with a smattering of bungalows and duplexes further inland. Among those beach hotels was the Halekulani, opened in 1917. Formerly a family home, it became a quaint gathering of cottages nestled in foliage fronting the unfortunately rather beachless coastline. But the lack of sand wasn't too tragic, because at the Halekulani you felt like you'd really found unhurried island living. The view of Diamond Head from the oceanfront of the Halekulani is the famous one seen on innumerable postcards.

The Moana Hotel, although crowded by modern Waikiki, still hangs onto its niche on the beach after 80 years. The Halekulani, alas, no longer survives in its original form.

Well-travelled: two relics of the Moana Hotel's long past - **(FACING PAGE)**, a baggage tag from the 1920's **(UPPER RIGHT)** and a brochure from around 1930, featuring some tasty looking ice cream-like mountains in the background **(LOWER RIGHT)**. Those fortunate enough to stay at the Halekulani Hotel in the early 1930's could slap a sticker like this one on their luggage **(LOWER LEFT)**, when the beach looked like this drawing in a <u>Paradise of the Pacific</u> magazine **(BELOW)**.

". . . who has not dreamed of living in a bungalow, under the coconut palms of Waikiki."

Halekulani Hotel brochure, 1926

ROYAL HAWAIIAN HOTEL

Unquestionably the big social event of 1927 was the opening of the Royal Hawaiian Hotel, which was more than just a grand society function. That's because it marked the start of a new era in Waikiki and tourism in general: the debut of the first great resort hotel in Hawaii. Previously, hotels had simply provided bed and board in pleasant surroundings and had let the visitor take care of himself. The Royal Hawaiian changed all that by offering a thousand and one things for you to do.

For example, there was archery, badminton, croquet, or tennis on both grass and paved courts. You could play "wee golf" right there on the hotel grounds or the regular-sized game at the affiliated Waialae Golf Course. Sightseeing or deep-sea fishing excursions and even ukulele lessons could be arranged through the hotel's own agencies. Smart shops with tasteful souvenirs and up-to-date fashions tempted you in the hotel lobby. Even just lying on the beach was different, for sunning in the special cordoned-off section of raked sand was where you saw "'nicer people' than in front of the Outrigger". When all this became tiresome, you could relax and let others entertain you — native boys would climb coconut palms for the benefit of your Kodak, and at dusk, the Royal Hawaiian Girls Glee Club would serenade beneath your window.

This resort concept is commonplace today, but in 1927 it was new and wonderful for a hotel in Hawaii to take such complete care of its guests. And what a hotel it was! "The longest lounge in any hotel anywhere, measuring 235 feet long . . . a battery of four high speed elevators . . . a huge porte cochere with two wide driveways for automobiles, thus avoiding any congestion of traffic . . . song birds singing happily in oddly designed and colored cages" and "a ballroom of Byzantine design" all set in the "splendid garden-paradise that surrounds the great hostelry" containing 200-year-old palms which "seem to have been placed just so". Wow! Little wonder, in the face of all this, that "passengers on ten world-cruise steamers" unanimously voted the Royal Hawaiian "The World's Most Beautiful Hotel."

The Royal stayed easily in its reigning position for decades, with an interruption during World War II as a military-held rest and recreation center. As Waikiki changed, though, its grandeur began to fade. The lush, well-tended gardens surrendered to development and today you can catch only a glimpse of a pink tower or two,

with a few "large deep-blue jardinieres or bowls placed appropriately on the roof" from between other buildings. Even in a diminished role, though, the Royal Hawaiian Hotel will still remain the exalted Pink Palace to many.

The Regal Royal: an artistic view on the cover of a booklet from the hotel's early years **(FACING PAGE)**, and one of a million postcards sent home by those who stayed there—or wished they had **(BELOW)**.

"If you're going to be very grand, go to the Royal Hawaiian Hotel. It's quite the last word, financially and otherwise. . ."

Highlights On Honolulu, 1930

Royal Hawaiian Hotel, Waikiki, T. H.

2B-H892

The Royal Hawaiian was the socially correct place for evening activities in the 1930's, with Harry Owens and his Royal Hawaiian Hotel Orchestra a leading attraction. Owens wrote songs (**LEFT**) and even invented dances, like the Oni-Oni, being demonstrated in 1934 (**FACING PAGE, NEAR RIGHT**) with Harry and the boys in the background. "Romancin' At The Royal" (record label, **BELOW**) is what these snappy couples are doing on the cover of a Royal Hawaiian menu (**FACING PAGE, FAR RIGHT**).

"The ballroom at the Royal Hawaiian Hotel acts as a potent magnet for sweet young things and their escorts."

Highlights On Honolulu, 1930

"*Postcards, too, in colors so shrill and false . . . the dark crimson sunset, the candy-pink Hawaiian dancer, and the acid-green grass of the pictured lawns.*"

Hawaii: Isles of Dreams, 1957

Not sending a postcard home from Hawaii would be absolutely unheard of. Not only do you want everyone back there to know you finally made that trip you always talked about, but they expect a card anyway. So you dutifully make the obligatory statements on the back of a postcard and send it off, just the way every other traveller always has.

Over the years the most popular postcard themes have stayed the same. As the quote says, the hula dancer (be she candy-pink or otherwise) has always been a favorite. Probably the only change in her appearance has been due to the shifts of fashion that affected all women's clothing: her skirt got shorter and her blouse became smaller until it eventually disappeared, leaving her topless.

Another favorite, and quite apart from such considerations, are the scenic splendors of Hawaii. Some of these natural views have stayed reassuringly similar through time, like the Pali Lookout on Oahu, while others have been changed by the intervention of man or nature. For example, you can't send a card of Onomea Arch on Hawaii anymore; it caved in some time ago. But old cards still preserve now-vanished scenes like this.

In addition there are things like a picture of your hotel (it's ok to draw an arrow pointing to where you stayed), or a luau, or a sunset, or surfers . . . in fact, all the images that are Hawaii in the public's mind. In a changing world, postcards still serve the same purpose they did decades ago.

Almost as necessary as postcard-sending while on your Hawaiian dream trip has always been the purchasing of souvenirs. Carved wooden tikis, ceramic cups with your name in Hawaiian, clear plastic paperweights containing sand and little fish; nowadays these and more compete for your attention at souvenir shops. But probably one item has always beaten them all: the aloha shirt, to be worn only occasionally once back home but always hanging there in the closet to bring back some nice memories. Return with us now to see how postcards and aloha shirts, the two perennial tourist purchases, have existed through the years.

(FACING PAGE): airmail stamp from 1952.

Having a wonderful time: postcards are absolutely essential to tourism, and with that being Hawaii's main occupation the assortment of cards has been understandably huge over the years. Sometimes the cards themselves were huge too, as Miss Mary Kearney found out in the late 1930's **(RIGHT)**. It's perhaps fortunate that most people didn't have to deal with postcards this size, since this giant greeting cost $10.50 to send via the new Pan American Hawaii Clipper. (Wonder what the message was?) For those who had to be content with more normal-sized cards, some special favorites stood out among the variety that was available. This fabric **(BELOW)** could be from anytime between 1937 and the mid-50's, and the postcards on it are all the best-known motifs of that era: a sunset, surfers with Diamond Head, and the beloved hula girl.

Wish you were here: to go with the fabric on the facing page, here are three actual postcards with the same favored illustrations. All date from the 1930's and '40's.

The aloha shirt is something that just about everybody knows. It's become a cliché by now, having been around for almost fifty years; the most obvious souvenir of Hawaii that anyone ever took home—"like a postcard you could wear", as one writer put it in 1953.

Where did all these wonderful designs come from? The mad jumble of things like Diamond Head and Aloha Tower, the garish and sometimes bizarre flowers, the strange fish entwined in undersea plants, the surfers and canoe paddlers and hula dancers, the palm trees, the ukuleles, the helpful Hawaiian words sprinkled throughout—in short, all the stereotypical Hawaiian images that make up this book—where did they all come from? Answer: from designers too numerous to name, even if they all were known, who were inspired by the beauties of Hawaii. The original ones actually worked in the islands, but later there were many others, employed by manufacturers in Japan and the U.S.A. who jumped on the bandwagon around 1950 when alohawear became an international craze.

It had all started some years before that, though. In the early 1930's, the more adventuresome members of a younger island-born generation began to appear in shirts they'd had made from brightly colored Japanese silks and cottons. Such fabric was traditionally used in Japan only for young children since its riotous hues were considered inappropriate for adults, but restrictions like these were ignored in Hawaii. By 1935 such shirts were a fad for young people of all races. Soon serious designers began to produce fabrics with Hawaiian themes, and the "aloha shirt" had arrived.

By 1939 the garment industry was flourishing, with much of its output intended for tourists. Local residents gradually took to this festive clothing too, helped by the invention of Aloha Week in 1947. During this yearly celebration of Hawaiian activities, every company urged its employees to sport the most brilliant alohawear they could find. The response was so enthusiastic that over the next decades such informality at work became the rule in Hawaii.

By the 1960's, the lavishly illustrated type of print with every possible Hawaiian motif thrown together had come to seem tacky and outdated, and manufacturers shunned it. But around 1970 such fabrics slowly began to creep back into style with the help (again) of the more adventuresome members of the younger and hipper set. This time the old shirts

were dubbed "silkies" (even though most were made of rayon), and they eventually became prized possessions. You only rarely find old silkies around anymore since most have passed through their second stage of usefulness by now—but when you do, their prices can be a shock for something that you could have bought for as little as 75¢ new in 1936!

A typical aloha shirt, (ABOVE) and a happy group of island girls all resplendent in their best muumuus, from the cover of a 1953 <u>Paradise of the Pacific</u> (FACING PAGE).

The alohawear era really began in 1936, when some local manufacturers got the bright idea of making ready-to-wear shirts for tourists who couldn't wait several days to have one tailormade. One such businessman, Ellery Chun, registered the term "aloha shirt" that year as a variation on the numerous other "aloha"-named items meant for tourists. Shown **(ABOVE)** is a later version of the historic clothing label that, in effect, named an entire industry. The name of Chun's store, King-Smith, is featured as the "creator" of the title.

Another pioneer in the field was George Brangier, seen with a female assistant **(UPPER RIGHT)** handling the then-new clothing craze. Brangier and his partner Nat Norfleet started their company, Branfleet,(later Kahala Sportswear) also in 1936. All the shirts in the photo are made from traditional Japanese cloth, the predecessor to the Hawaiian-designed fabric that would appear around 1937.

". . . shirts . . in exotic prints, over which tumble in delightful confusion tropical fish and palm trees, Diamond Head and the Aloha Tower, surfboards and leis, ukuleles and Waikiki beach scenes."

The Honolulu Advertiser, 1939

BEN STUDIOS

Aloha ... Hawaii !

KAMEHAMEHA
made and styled in
HAWAII

Made and styled in Hawaii: The Kamehameha Garment Company is another oldtimer in the land of alohawear, having gotten in on the ground floor in 1936. The ad at right, from 1947, was intended to introduce mainland customers to playclothes made of "famed fabrics that thrive on sun and water."

Alohawear's popularity outside of Hawaii peaked in the 1950's when even mainland manufacturers were designing "Hawaiian" print sportshirts. Frequent publicity regarding Hawaii's attempts to gain statehood all through the decade probably helped to make people aware of the islands and their fashions, but movies undoubtedly played a bigger role. "From Here To Eternity" dressed its principal male actors like Frank Sinatra and Ernest Borgnine in a succession of aloha shirts that more accurately reflected the fashions of the year the film was made (1954) than the year in which it was set (1941).

"To arrive in Hawaii . . . and then to switch abruptly into one of those kaleidoscopic shirts in violent reds and wild blues and insane yellows - that is no procedure for a sensitive man to follow."

Waikiki Beachnik, 1960

A tense scene in "From Here To Eternity" takes place between "hostess" (in the book, prostitute) Donna Reed and angry soldier Montgomery Clift **(LEFT)**, clad of course in the necessary tropical print shirt. The one he wears at the end of the film, when he's lying dead in a sandtrap at the Waialae Golf Course, is even nicer.

More film fabric: John Wayne, hard-hitting Federal G-man on the trail of communists in Hawaii, questions a suspect's blonde land-lady in "Big Jim McLain" (1952). That's a detail of the same fabric she's wearing **(FAR RIGHT)**, if you wanted a closer look.

"Meanwhile... with your hearth as a port of departure, and easy-chair for a ship... sail with us on a word-and-picture voyage to mid-Pacific..."

Nearby Hawaii, 1934

The main reason for promoting Hawaii is to lure visitors to the islands. Promotion can take various forms, but the most effective is the direct advertising of Hawaii in magazines and brochures. In such a case, a hard sell really isn't appropriate, since the intent of the ad is to create in you a feeling for the beauty of the islands—and to make you, the prospective tourist, want to see these delights for yourself. Thus, prices are seldom mentioned. Neither are comparisons made with other vacation spots, nor claims that Hawaii gives more fun for the money. More important are the "intangibles", such as the friendliness and comeliness of the people, the romance and excitement you'll encounter, and so on.

Taking care of these advertising needs today is the Hawaii Visitors Bureau, the latest in a long line of assorted promotional agencies that stretch back in time to the early 1900's. The Bureau and its predecessors have played a key job not only in handling requests for information from all over the world, but also in overseeing the work of whatever company is producing Hawaii's direct advertising. In terms of the total amount of promotion, such work by the HVB has been overshadowed for some time by that released by private business concerns, such as hotel chains, airlines, and (in the past) steamship companies.

Social and economic changes have been reflected in Hawaii's direct advertising. The typical visitor of the pre-war decades tended to be wealthy and with lots of time to spend on vacation. But as ships were replaced by planes, and more people gained the money to travel, the upper-class aim of the ads of the 1930's was superceded by a push more towards the general populace. This change has given the older advertising about Hawaii a nostalgic look and tone that will never be seen again - because the islands' reliance on that kind of wealthier tourist will probably never happen again.

(FACING PAGE): <u>Nearby Hawaii</u>, a Hawaii Tourist Bureau booklet, 1934.

irect advertising of Hawaii has changed over the years in the same manner as all advertising has. Shown here are the typically undefined and almost hazy illustrations that were common before World War II—illustrations suggesting, rather than shouting, that Hawaii is wonderfully romantic. The now almost-total use of photography in advertising (a switch that took place during the 1950's) has driven such artwork from the pages of magazines and brochures. Although a good photo is able to induce a romantic mood, it can probably never be as evocative as these illustrations are.

"Decades of advertising have convinced practically every stranger outside the islands that Hawaii is still a semi-civilized Eden . . . where Polynesian girls go about in ti-leaf skirts and do the hula."

Fortune magazine, 1940

The hula girl spotlit on the beach at Waikiki **(RIGHT)** is from 1931; Hawaii was "only" a week away then (by ship, of course). **(FACING PAGE)**: this is the type of night-life you could expect in 1934, undoubtedly at the Royal Hawaiian Hotel: natives playing music, smart couples, the happy presentation of a lei. Isn't all that enough to convince you that it's "time to stop 'JUST PLANNING' a trip to Hawaii"?

time to stop "JUST PLANNING" a trip to *Hawaii*

Hawaii wasn't just advertised for itself, for it could be helpful in selling other things too. Apart from companies that directed their Hawaiian connections to tourists—how to get there, where to stay, which automobile to rent—there were others who used the islands as an alluring backdrop for their products. It was an example of how people and their needs were the same all over, for even in exotic Hawaii they still drove cars and used telephones. Island residents enjoyed an American standard of living like the rest of the country, but their endorsement of a product could add a bit of glamor to what might be a pretty unexciting and everyday item.

On the other hand, utilizing products from Hawaii could bring a touch of the desirable tropics into your own home. We've already seen how the pineapple growers suggested this to add some prestige and excitement to their already tasty fruit; here a 1925 newspaper ad printed in Hawaii **(RIGHT)** informs the populace that the pineapple growers are not just advertising their products but all of Hawaii as well—to the benefit of everybody in the islands.

How **HAWAII** is being advertised by The **ASSOCIATION** of **HAWAIIAN PINEAPPLE CANNERS**

81 Advertisements - 12 Million Homes
- 384 Million Advertising Sales Messages

The name and fame of Hawaii is carried into millions of American homes every year by the extensive advertising and publicity campaigns of the Hawaiian Pineapple industry. Brilliantly colored illustrated advertisements are carried continuously in all the leading women's magazines of the country, telling the story of Hawaiian Pineapple and the picturesque, smiling country where it is grown.

The growth of the Hawaiian Pineapple industry has been accomplished in a large measure through this consistent advertising and sales effort.

Aloha in the ads: a pretty Hawaiian girl might make a phone call like anyone else in the U.S.A. in 1942 **(FAR RIGHT)**, but this ad suggests rather improbably that she'd be speaking Hawaiian. In fact, under the martial law that was ruling Hawaii at that time, all telephone calls had to be in English. **(NEAR RIGHT):** these GI's and their local friends are enjoying Cokes in 1945; the illustration is apt, since Maui was inundated (like the other islands) with thousands of military personnel during World War II.

'Eia ke ola...Have a Coke
(HERE'S HEALTH)

...or winning a welcome in Wailuku

Here's health is the happy expression of Hawaiian hospitality. Just as friendly is the *Have a Coke* of the Army flyer. In these three words he says *We're pals*. On a Hawaiian beach, where fishermen toss their nets in the sea...just as in your own home...Coca-Cola brings friendly refreshment to all comers. In Wailuku or Wichita, Coca-Cola stands for *the pause that refreshes,*—has become a symbol of a friendly way of living. Keep Coke on hand in your refrigerator—for your family and your guests.

*   *   *

Our fighting men meet up with Coca-Cola many places overseas, where it's bottled on the spot. Coca-Cola has been a globe-trotter "since way back when".

Coca-Cola
REG. U.S. PAT. OFF.
-the global high-sign

Coke = Coca-Cola
It's natural for popular names to acquire friendly abbreviations. That's why you hear Coca-Cola called Coke.

COPYRIGHT 1945, THE COCA-COLA COMPANY

"Aloha au ia oukou," *she said*
— *with the help of a lump of coal*

Ask her what she's doing, and she'll say she is talking to distant dear ones, saying, "My love to you all," if you *must* know.

Ask a Koppers chemist what she's doing, and (because he eats and sleeps with coal on his mind) he'd say: "She's holding a handset made of a phenol plastic... and phenol comes from a lump of coal." And he might add: "Underground cables that carry her message are wrapped in burlap which is impregnated with a coal tar saturant. Another job for coal to do."

If you didn't stop him, he might remind you of all the telephone poles that are pressure-treated with creosote. And tell you how creosote comes from coal.

Plenty of articles we use every day get a helping hand from coal. Printing inks and pipe coatings, sulfapyridine and fruit sprays, waterproofing and mothballs, vitamins and varnishes...chemicals from coal contribute to all of these.

Koppers chemists are constantly seeking hidden treasures to be found in coal. These treasures are hard to extract, hard to make commercially available. But much has been accomplished...and more wonders lie ahead in chemicals from coal. Write for list of free Koppers technical literature. Koppers Company, 1106 Koppers Building, Pittsburgh.

Koppers is an important factor in the mining, treating, processing, construction, manufacturing and transportation industries. In 36 out of 48 states you will find Koppers activities.

Chemicals from Coal

The travel brochure exists to present Hawaii's many charms to those across the sea who have yet to discover the whole delightful affair. Picked up in an idle moment at a travel agency, the brochure can begin to work its magic once the prospective visitor is settled comfortably at home. With diverting photos and poetic prose, John Q. Public soon finds the view of his own backyard pretty dreary when he could be seeing something a lot more exciting. And so, as soon as he can afford it, Mr. Public and wife and kiddies are off for the Paradise of the Pacific.

Did it really work this way? Undoubtedly yes. To catch the fancy of those who might be thinking of taking a trip—but hadn't yet decided where—Hawaii needed full-time promotional workers, and by the 1920's the Hawaii Tourist Bureau was rolling along, with the assistance of private business concerns who were hyping Hawaii too. They all happily churned out brochures of every size and shape to spread the message throughout the land that Hawaii was the place to vacation and perhaps even settle down to live (if you had a skill that was in demand, that is, and firm job prospects before you left home. No new beachcombers needed, thank you.) The way to lure 'em out here was to make things sound exotic but still comfortably familiar. It helped to say that Hawaii was part of the United States (a basic fact many are still unaware of) where people spoke English and used the same money and served normal food. No fussy tourist was going to go someplace which didn't have all the necessities for keeping body and soul together.

"Eden of peace and pleasure. Lotus isles of love and laziness. The loveliest fleet of islands that lies anchored in any ocean. No fogs, no hurricanes, no poisonous plants. Tropical fruits you can enjoy without limit, water you can drink with safety, and plumbing that is American." All this and American plumbing too!

Send for free illustrated booklet: **(FACING PAGE),** a very early effort from 1910 **(NEAR LEFT),** "Hawaii/Fine Anytime" from the 1920's **(FAR LEFT),** and a multi-page booklet that covers just about everything you ever wanted to know about Hawaii but were afraid to ask, from 1925 **(RIGHT).**

"Languid nights of ecstatic romance . . . turbulent days of roaring, blistering excitement beyond the white man's last barrier! Pagan love . . . primitive hate . . . unforgettable drama!"

Advertisement for "Aloma of the South Seas", 1941

Hawaii is closer to Hollywood than you might think. In the glory days of the studio system, films of every genre and quality were made about Hawaii. Of course, not all of them were actually filmed in the islands; usually the most that Hollywood could manage were a few scenes shot on location to serve as backdrops for action that would take place later on soundstages back in the film capital.

Any type of story-line might be set in Hawaii. Musicals, for example, were perfect for the island treatment since they relied on song and romance, both of which Hawaii offered in abundance. Included among the battalions of hula dancers could be, for example, tap dancer Eleanor Powell, doing a jazzed-up hula in "Honolulu" (1939), or child singing prodigy Bobby Breen in "Hawaii Calls" (1938). Mysteries and spy stories? How about Evelyn Keyes searching for her long-lost husband through the seamier parts of downtown Honolulu in "Hell's Half Acre" (1953), or John Wayne and James Arness uncovering a communist plot to disrupt local shipping in "Big Jim McLain" (1952). In another vein altogether would be comedies like "Abbott and Costello In The Navy" (1941) and its reworking ten years later,

"Sailor Beware", with that decade's big comedy team, Dean Martin and Jerry Lewis. (In both cases, the Navy shipped the boys off to Hawaii). Along with these we must include 1955's "Ma and Pa Kettle At Waikiki". And if that film doesn't sound scary enough, there was Boris Karloff among his man-eating plants on "Voodoo Island" (better know as the island of Kauai) from 1957, to represent the horror movie category.

The point of all this is clear: Hollywood's use of Hawaii for all these decades has created the public's most vivid and widespread impression of the islands. Nowadays producers of TV shows are using Hawaii more than film studios are. But the islands' appeal for audiences remains the same as ever—and probably will continue for a long time to come.

(FACING PAGE): movie crew filming at Waikiki, 1931.

by colored lights and edged with metal plaques bearing the signatures of Hollywood's biggest stars of the 1930's, while in the frescoed lobby waited usherettes garbed in uniforms based on the clothing of Hawaiian royalty. Inside, you were (and still are) surrounded by the illusion of a huge tropical garden lined by verdant foliage, with moving clouds projected realistically on the ceiling and a rainbow-arched screen flanked by two life-sized bogus coconut palms. They sure don't build 'em like that anymore!

Spectacle of the screen: while it was exotica for everyone else, island moviegoers had fun watching "Hawaiian" movies to see themselves as others saw them. But just like the rest of the country, local audiences were treated to some pretty grand structures to view these films in. Downtown Honolulu's Hawaii Theater, for example, was fairly ornate and boasted the most spectacular neon marquee in the islands. It's shown here crowded with sailors in 1946 (UPPER LEFT). More classy was the wonderful Waikiki Theater, built in 1936 (LOWER RIGHT). A fountain in its courtyard was lit

Topic of the tropics: when a film about Hawaii came to town advertisements invariably flaunted the local angle, correctly assuming that everyone would want to see Hollywood's latest Hawaiian fantasy to check its authenticity. "Hawaiian Nights" **(ABOVE)**, appeared in 1939, while the far-fetched "Waikiki Wedding" **(LEFT)**, was an early attraction at—where else?—the equally fanciful Waikiki Theater.

Hooray for Hollywood's version of Hawaii! Shown here and on the following pages, a smattering of the many films with a Hawaiian setting produced by the dream factory over the years. **(ABOVE)**: an invented island scene re-created on a studio soundstage — the pagan part of the "Little Hula Heaven" number from "Waikiki Wedding" (1937).

The most durable story of native love and all that stuff is "Bird of Paradise", which bears much of the responsibility for introducing Hawaii into American popular culture. When it first appeared as a Broadway stage presentation in 1912 it inspired a Hawaiian music craze that lasted for years. The tale

came to the screen for the first time in 1932 and starred Joel McCrea and Delores Del Rio **(FACING PAGE, UPPER LEFT)**. "Bird of Paradise" made a second and grander showing in 1951 (other two photos), and this time Louis Jourdan was the foreign interloper brought back to the islands by native Jeff Chandler. Louis, after much soul-searching and some stern warnings from his buddy, decides he'll stay and marry Jeff's sister Kalua (played by Debra Paget - another "ethnic" actress). The evilminded old kahuna doesn't care for this arrangement, and after making Debra walk over hot coals **(UPPER RIGHT)** he decides she must jump into the angrily erupting volcano. She does, the vol-

cano quiets down, and Louis goes home brokenhearted. Yes, that really is Hawaii in the background; the 1951 production was filmed on location. Do you suppose yet another version will be made someday?

"Bird of Paradise": ill-fated lovers Luana and Johnny share a tender moment before they are cruelly parted forever (1932, **ABOVE**), Kalua takes a sizzling stroll, **(UPPER RIGHT)**, and mass panic erupts as the volcano gets angry (both 1951, **RIGHT**).

Rhythm of the islands: during the heyday of the musical film, Hawaii inspired a number of stars to burst into song.

Bing Crosby handles a gift (the duck) in the matrimonial scene that opens 1937's "Waikiki Wedding" **(BELOW)**. No, Bing's not getting married, he's just there to sing for the newlyweds. This lighthearted romp has to do with a mainland girl, Shirley Ross, who's brought to Hawaii as the winner of a contest sponsored by a pineapple company. She's unimpressed with paradise ("To me, it's just Birch Falls with a lot of palm trees stuck in it") and advertising man Bing, who had the bright idea for the contest in the first place, is called in to show Shirley a good time to counteract the bad press she's giving the islands. To

do this he concocts a false kidnapping scheme that spirits Shirley away to an old-timey native village. She eventually falls for both Hawaii and Bing, and tells her stuffy fiancé to go back home to Birch Falls. Everyone gets to sing lots of songs, and the best known of them turned out to be "Sweet Leilani", the Harry Owens composition that was not only a huge hit but an Oscar winner too.

Can island-born Betty Grable successfully reintegrate back into a society where they've "never heard of Jell-O or of Abbott and Costello"? She's going to try in "Song of the Islands" (1942), having returned home and brought Victor Mature and Jack Oakie back with her from the land across the sea **(ABOVE)**. Island entertainer Hilo Hattie also played a role in this movie, one of her many such appearances. Betty's Dad

Europe (art imitates life). Instead he becomes a tour guide ("Why, I know these islands like I know the back of mah own hand!") whose first personally conducted tour is this group of "high school girls" and their teacher. The blonde on the far right turns out to be the main troublemaker who causes most of the film's complications; after a good spanking on the beach from Elvis she stops being snotty and becomes as sweet as sugar. Plenty of lively musical numbers occur, including the immortal "Rock-A-Hula Baby". All ends happily as Elvis marries his faithful girlfriend in a lavish ceremony at the Coco Palms Hotel on Kauai, complete with floating wedding barge.

still lives in the tropics and has long been seized by Polynesian paralysis, unlike his daughter when she's leading her chorus group through an extremely energetic dance performance (ABOVE), cellophane hula skirts and all. "Song of the Islands" bore the misfortune of terrible timing since it was released in early 1942, only a month or so after the Pearl Harbor tragedy. No one wanted to be reminded of the Pacific when it seemed that all the news coming from there was scary, and the film did poorly.

(RIGHT): Elvis Presley shows his shapely charges how to paddle out to catch the big ones in "Blue Hawaii" (1961), his most popular film and the first of three he made on location in the islands. The "Big E" plays a local resident who refuses to go into the family pineapple business after his return home from a stint with the Army in

Hollywood on holiday: hardworking movie stars needed rest too, and Hawaii was the perfect spot for some relaxation "before my next picture begins shooting". An island vacation could also be a helpful publicity boost for Hawaii itself when photos of filmdom's well-known travellers were released for printing all over the country. Can you identify these famous folk out of costume and without makeup?

This page: **(RIGHT)**, that's Charlie Chaplin without his moustache but with lots of leis at dockside in 1917. The comedy star made a big splash during his visit with a brief but funny session as a stand-in traffic cop in downtown Honolulu's main intersection. The lovely young lady with Charlie is starlet Edna Purviance. **(LOWER RIGHT)**: operatic songstress Jeanette McDonald happily takes a cookie offered by a little hula girl in the late 1930's. **(BELOW LEFT)**: say the magic word and win a hundred dollars—like Charlie, above, Groucho Marx is also lacking his famous moustache as he arrives in the late 1930's.

For some time there was a strong market for publicity pictures of film stars which movie studios and others were happy to fill. One such local agency was the Pan-Pacific Press Bureau, which in the late 1930's recorded incidents like Spencer Tracy **(LEFT)** giving an autograph the Hawaiian way, on a coconut held by a young fan on Waikiki Beach. **(LOWER LEFT)**: not in the water but close to it is swimmer/ movie star Esther Williams, taking a break from the filming of "Pagan Love Song" on location in 1950,' with her husband and little son. **(LOWER RIGHT)**: he may have been skinny but he sure could sing —Frank Sinatra caused feminine hearts to pound when he visited in 1947.

Aloha on the air: this 1936 sheet music (LEFT) graphically shows what happens "When Hawaii Calls" from the middle of the Pacific all the way to the mainland U.S.A. The recording of the theme song of another national radio program (BELOW) is from the same time.

awaii was well served by radio. Ordinary people of the 1920's and 30's were exposed for the first time to the sounds of the world's faraway places (like Hawaii), and they liked it. The programs they heard from paradise typically included lovely Hawaiian music, the haunting native language being spoken, and lots of evocative descriptions of the many beauties of the isles. Radio's strong point has always been that it demands the use of the listener's imagination to picture what it is talking about, and this worked very much in favor of Hawaii as the announcer told of being right on the beach at Waikiki with the warm waves lapping the sand almost at the base of the stage itself, the blue skies above, and the tradewinds in the palm trees overhead. There's no question that the nights spent dreaming by the radio as it spoke of paradise and played soft tunes of the islands inspired many to make the trip to alohaland to see all this for themselves. The utilization of predominately live entertainment on both local and national radio shows also provided steady and secure employment for musicians, thus keeping that segment of the arts lively and healthy.

In addition to programs actually emanating from Hawaii itself, there were shows featuring Hawaiian performers appearing on the mainland in various locations like hotel ballrooms, for these were the days of the live remote broadcasts: "Ladies and gentlemen, we take you now to the Lexington Hotel in New York City . . . " But the most influential and longest-lived Hawaiian radio program was "Hawaii Calls", run by the tireless Webley Edwards. It was broadcast from the islands from 1935 to 1975 and was heard over hundreds of stations at the height of its success. A transition to television in the 1960's did not do as well, though. Perhaps you needed the element of imagination that radio provided.

Songbirds of Hawaii: all dressed up in their best flowery holokus are the members of the Bina Mossman Glee Club, ready to perform in the KGU studio in 1939 **(ABOVE).**

Index

Credits

All items pictured are from the following sources:

Bernice P. Bishop Museum
DeSoto Brown
Rita Cole
Anne Ellett
Jack and Marty Ford
Gary Giemza
Hawaii State Archives

Hawaiian Music Foundation
Arthur Johnsen
Keep 'Em Flying, Seattle
Marcus Lee
Don Severson
Harry Soria Jr.

Thank yous
To the collectors who allowed us to photograph their treasures, especially Jack and Marty Ford . . .
To the helpful people at the Hawaii State Archives and the Bishop Museum, especially in the Photo Collection . . .
For other assistance: Jim Bigwood, Jerry Hopkins, Dave Rick, and the late Andy Riley, who gave us our name . . .
And most of all, to the outstanding artists who created the dream paradise of Hawaii.

Photo credits:
Bernice P. Bishop Museum: 14 (bottom right), 39 (lower right), 54, 73 (right), 75 (right), 89 (right), 91 (left), 118 (right), 120, 122 (top), 123 (left).
Hawaii State Archives: 38, 55 (lower right), 70 (right), 81 (left), 104 (top), 108 (right), 128 (all), 129 (upper and lower left).

DeSoto Brown was born in the Territory of Hawaii in 1954, a fourth-generation islander of part-Hawaiian ancestry. He began collecting a very wide range of 20th century Hawaiiana—from license plates to aloha shirts—at the age of thirteen, and at one time had his own radio show, "Melodies of Paradise", which utilized his old Hawaiian 78rpm discs. DeSoto's strong interest in popular culture eventually led him into the research and writing of Hawaii Recalls.

Anne Ellett is a Honolulu-based graphic designer born in Japan who has lived in Hawaii for the past two decades. While working as an art director at a Honolulu advertising agency she developed a fondness for Hawaii's colorful graphic arts past through involvement in present-day advertising campaigns.

Gary Giemza was born in Philadelphia in 1951 and knew very little about the islands until he saw a copy of a comic book called "Dennis the Menace in Hawaii" in 1960. After graduating from the Tyler School of Fine Art, he moved to Hawaii in 1973 and became an enthusiastic local resident. An artist by trade, Gary photographed most of the objects pictured in this book over a four year period.

photography (this page): Nicholas LaFratta, Richard Peterson